Outsourcing
100 Success Secrets

Outsourcing 100 Success Secrets - 100 Most
Asked Questions: The Missing IT, Business
Process, Call Center, HR- Outsourcing to India,
China and more Guide

Gerard Blokdijk

Outsourcing 100 Success Secrets

Copyright © 2008 by Gerard Blokdijk

Outsourcing 100 Success Secrets
Gerard Blokdijk

There has never been an Outsourcing Guide like this.

100 Success Secrets is *not* about the ins and outs of Outsourcing. Instead, it answers the top 100 questions that we are asked and those we come across in forums, our consultancy and education programs. It tells you exactly how to deal with those questions, with tips that have never before been offered in print.

This book is also *not* about Outsourcing's best practice and standards details. Instead, it introduces everything you want to know to be successful with Outsourcing.

Table of Contents

Tips in Choosing The Best Accounting Outsourcing

Accounting outsourcing is among the most popular areas of company outsourcing. More small and medium size businesses use this because it is time consuming and difficult. In this way, companies can focus more on the important or core functions of the company. There are several advantages in availing of accounting outsourcing. Aside from relieving the company of the tedious job of accounting and bookkeeping, it can also save some operational costs such as office space and other operational costs.

Before venturing into accounting outsourcing, a company has to keep in mind some tips before making the decision: First, the company must make sure that the outsourcing company is reliable and dependable. Accounting and bookkeeping is a tedious and sensitive job, therefore, certified professionals and staffs are needed. The company must check on the qualifications of the staff and the references provided by the outsourcing company. Second, the company must make clear what its expectations are to the outsourcing company.

It is very important that goals and deliverables are clearly outlined to avoid confusion. Third, the company must ask the accounting company about past projects that they have done. Doing this shall give the company an idea about the working attitude of the accounting company. To be more sure, the company might want to start new with small projects and see from there. The above tips are just a few of the many things that a company should keep in mind when hiring an accounting outsourcing company. Keep in mind that a company avails of outsourcing to make the company more successful therefore being careful and critical to choosing a good accounting outsourcing company is the first step towards it

Advantages of Outsourcing: Why Outsourcing?

The outsourcing market is expected to grow more in the coming years. Many companies are becoming aware of the potentials and advantages inherent in outsourcing.

This is due to the experiences of many companies in outsourcing, which makes them more aware of the risks and potentials. Although there are the disadvantages such as non-loyalty and other vested interests of outsourcing companies, the advantages are far greater.

1. Outsourcing saves operational costs. Saving operational costs can come in two ways.

First, a company can avail of world-class technology at lower rates. Outsourcing companies, which already has the resources and expertise, can save the company a lot of money. Second, the company saves on skilled manpower at lower rates than hiring internal staff. Outsourcing companies offer skilled manpower at lower rates, which can make savings for the company as well as increase productivity.

2. Improvement on Core Business Areas

Outsourcing can also make companies concentrate more on the core functions of the business, thereby making it more successful. Back operations businesses may be outsourced and managed by another company, instead of including them among the core business areas.

3. Outsourcing can be used to develop internal staff. Outsourcing can also be used as a tool to develop the internal employees. The internal employees are important because they are aware of the interest of the company and are more loyal, therefore a company must also think about their development.

First, due to outsourcing, internal employees have more time to pursue development efforts for the company such as policy making. Secondly, the consultants and experts from the outsourcing company can train the internal staff. The advantages of outsourcing far outweigh the disadvantages. Knowing the advantages can make the company aware of the potentials of entering into this venture and capitalizing on them.

American Outsourcing: What are its Effects on the American Economy?

Outsourcing happens when a company subcontracts another company to do its other business functions. This has been done by the Americans to reduce operational costs and also tap experts from other countries.

The common outsourcing functions are customer service, document management and telemarketing. Countries that are major outsourcers are India and China because they provide labor at much reduced rates. Statistics show that outsourcing is on the rise. Estimates by the McKinsey Global Institute shows that the increase can be as much as 30 to 40 percent a year for the next five years. Other studies also estimate that approximately 3 million jobs shall be moved overseas by 2015.

Americans are starting to worry about these figures. What are the Effects of Outsourcing? It was said that the industries that shall suffer from American outsourcing should be those in the financial services and information technology. Since the labor is cheaper in other countries, companies would opt to avail of out-sourcing as a cost reduction strategy.

However, this idea is making the Americans worry about the future. Does this mean that massive job losses shall occur in the future? Are there negative effects to the American economy due to outsourcing? There is no need to worry. It was said that most of the figures and statistics shown are just estimates. In reality, offshore outsourcing is very minimal compared to the size of the entire American economy.

Moreover, although there are more jobs offered outside of the US instead of being offered internally does not mean that this has a negative effect on the American economy. More outsourcing means more companies are thriving which in turn is good for the entire economy. American outsourcing is one of the products of globalization, which have been advantages to other countries. However, the Americans need not worry that they are losing jobs, but instead look at this as a thriving business that is mutually beneficial for Americans and other countries as well.

Application Outsourcing:

Application outsourcing as defined by bitpipe.com is the deployment, management and upgrades of packaged or customized software that is contracted out to an external provider. Today, due to the massive volume of data, companies are opting to find application outsourcing companies. However, there is always the question of security. Some companies think twice before entrusting their data to an outsource company. A company is under pressure to save cost and at the same time increase productivity, and then it has to know some tips on how to choose a good application outsourcing company.

1. What kind of outsourcing does the company need? There are many options to choose from depending on the scale. If email is needed then hosting is better. Managed services may be the best choice if a company has to scale among different countries or regions.

2. Are there hidden costs? Would the option to outsource incur more operational costs than what was expected? If yes, better think twice. A good example is in the case of collocation where the company has to think of additional expenses such as staffing, office space rents and others. There are also hidden fees from providers, which the company should know in advance.

3. Do the services come with guarantees? Companies should know whether providers could give guarantees in cases of problems. Guarantees can also help in customer retention.

4. Does the provider provide support when the company needs it? The company should make sure that there are available representatives every time in cases of problems. Application out-

sourcing is not an easy decision for a company especially if they are handling sensitive data. But choosing the right one and asking the important questions can make a big difference.

What are the Benefits of Outsourcing?

The main reason why outsourcing is on the rise is that companies -- may it be small or large businesses-- are attracted to the reduction of operational cost that outsourcing entails. However, companies should not be tunneled vision to look at this as a way to cut costs. Seeing a larger picture can spell a difference to whether outsourcing can work for a company or not. Many businesses do not understand the full extent of the benefits of outsourcing. While it can cut costs, it also has lots of benefits.

1.Outsourcing can increase efficiency because outsourcing companies better does some functions. These companies might have the technical expertise and resources to do such functions at a lower cost. Lower cost means that you can make your services and products competitively priced in the market.

2. Outsourcing can reduce labor cost. The savings from labor can be used for the personnel development of your in-house employees, which is an effective management strategy.

3. Outsourcing means that a company can make investments into more revenue-producing activities. Investors shall then see this as a good sign.

4. Outsourcing can help the company to start a project as soon as possible. This is possible because the outsourcing company has the resources and the expertise to handle the project immediately. Unlike in-house projects, there is no need to take weeks or months for training and support services.

5. For small businesses, outsourcing can be beneficial for them because they can save a lot of money and enjoy the same level of efficiency and expertise that large companies have. Outsourcing can also be viewed as a leveling instrument in the playing field. Outsourcing is not just to cut costs; it can also enhance efficiency, effectiveness and level the playing field for small businesses.

BPO Outsourcing: Is This For All Companies?

What is BPO? Business Process Outsourcing or BPO is the process of hiring an outsourcing company to provide services that a company should and could normally do. Before, BPO consists only of payroll services but now it also includes a number of functions such as financial and administration, human resources, customer services and accounting services.

Often, the outsourcing contracts between a company and the partner outsource company involves many years and millions of dollars. What are the basic know-how s for companies? A company before entering into outsourcing arrangements should know some basic knowledge about this. There is a right way to approach BPO.

1. A company should be aware that outsourcing has cycles and each cycle involves strategies. Using Gartner s outsourcing model, four phases are identified. These are sourcing strategy, evaluation and selection, contract development and sourcing management. The company management should ask itself questions on each of this strategy such as the risks and the reasons behind all the actions he has to make.

2. A company must know the duration of the contract. Usually, BPO contracts last from three to five years. The company must be able to make a balance, making it long enough to produce results and short enough to easily make changes.

3. A company must be able to make identification and assessment of the risks involved in outsourcing. The main idea here is to be able to separate the functions that can be outsourced and those that must remain in-house. There are many processed that

can be delegated but there are those that involves much risk such as policymaking and accountability. There are still many issues that a company has to evaluate before entering BPO outsourcing. Being aware of these is the first step. The next step is applying these to your company.

The Disadvantages of the Business Outsourcing Trend

In this day and age, outsourcing business processes to third-party companies has been the trend that almost every company is trying to emulate. Though outsourcing is indeed a business strategy that works for some companies, there are also some unexpected drawbacks associated with it. This is the reason why a lot of negative criticisms have been thrown to outsourcing in terms of (a) language skills, (b) quality of service, and (c) security.

When outsourcing is combined with off-shoring to regions with different language and culture, expect that dissatisfaction from customers will come in. This happens mostly in call centers wherein English may not be the primary language. Customers are having difficulties understanding call center agents due to variations in accent, word usage and sentence construction. Though product knowledge may be excellent, language barrier is undoubtedly one of the factors that lead to conflicts and misunderstandings.

If there is communication gap, quality of service is at stake as well. Another factor is that since the main purpose of outsourcing is to reduce costs, other services may be put in jeopardy due to lack of necessary resources. Though questionnaires may measure quality of service rendered, an unbiased Service Level Agreement (SLA) should still be prioritized to clearly define the necessary deliverables for each business process.

Security has always been an issue related with outsourcing. The company may not have the capacity to control each and every transaction done by the third-party company, therefore resulting to some legal security and compliance issues. There are even staff members from the third-party company who were penalized because of getting the most out of being exposed to confidential company and customer information. This is indeed one of the areas of outsourcing that needs to be addressed as well.

Business Process Outsourcing Learning the Basic Concept of BPO s

Getting into the Business Process Outsourcing (BPO) trend also means acquiring a third-party company in which the transmission of company services with its associated operational activities and responsibilities will take place. This is yet another business strategy with certain expectations to meet such as providing services with at least a guaranteed equal service level so as to avoid client-customer conflicts. BPO indeed provides definite solutions to companies while promising more efficient organizational designs as a result of productivity growth, cost reduction and innovative competencies.

Currently, BPO is divided into two categories: (a) back-office outsourcing and (b) front-office outsourcing. If back-office outsourcing deals with internal business functions such as payroll and human resources, front-office outsourcing, on the other hand, includes customer-related functions such as tech support through phone, chat or email. These categories are further subdivided into three, namely

(a) inshore outsourcing

(b) nearshore outsourcing and

(c) offshore outsourcing, depending on the BPO location. Inshore outsourcing means that the BPO company contracted is within a company s own country. If the contracted BPO is located on a company s neighboring country, then this is called nearshore outsourcing. Once the BPO company contracted is located outside the company s own country, it is then an offshore outsourcing.

There are also certain risks involved to acquiring BPO services. This is because it is more like transferring all business elements including process management, software and people to a third-party company on behalf of the outsourcer. Risks should be carefully managed to successfully achieve desired benefits. Otherwise, this will only lead to failing of company expectations, therefore business growth and development will be at stake.

The Truth Behind Call Center Outsourcing

The customer is always right   this is a common statement instilled to a lot of employees who get to interact customers or clients each and every working day. This is because it is through only excellent customer service that people get more value for their money. This is also the reason why many companies are investing on training so that their employees will be given a chance to improve their customer service abilities and get to meet or even exceed customer expectations. A very good ingredient that adds more color to every customer interaction is having exceptional communication skills. In the call center industry, this is one of the main areas that are being focused on.

Though large companies have the capacity to establish their own call centers, some resort to outsourcing their call center needs. This is what makes call center outsourcing a critical part of any business operation. However, it is a must to assess first if going to the call center outsourcing direction is indeed what the business needs. Some of these reasons would most likely due to low costs.

Given that a call center specializes in phone support and is acquired by most companies simply mean that good management is in place. Therefore it is just a good business strategy to acquire their services, without the need to spend time in hiring qualified individuals, and purchasing extra resources. In short, the business saves more money rather than starting from scratch.

Indeed, it would be a smart move to conduct researches first and analyze what the specific needs of the business are before making that most important decision. Call center outsourcing companies have their own specialization and choosing the best bet will yield more desirable results in the future.

Outsourcing in China   Good or Bad Move

One of the questions being asked in the four corners of the outsourcing world is this   Will China rule the future of outsourcing? The answer is yet to be determined as there are still a lot of Asian players that are indeed doing well in as far as growth and progress in terms of acquiring outsourcing jobs is concerned. Two of the countries that provide competition to China include India and the Philippines. Without a doubt, these countries have already established their competence and credibility in the world of outsourcing.

Now, what makes China a potential candidate? First and foremost, it has a large labor supply pool like what India has. In addition, companies who have setup Asian headquarters can avail of China s bilingual population. Most people can speak both Japanese and Chinese, particularly in key cities such as Shanghai. Aside from this, people in China are known to be hardworking and very much dedicated in any line of work. They produce quality work just like any other nationality, provided that proper training is given.

How about China s disadvantage? One is that most Chinese people do not have good English language capabilities. Second is lack of project management expertise, which is very much critical in today business world.

Salary-wise, this is not much of an issue. Research shows that though programmer costs in China is about 10 to 15% lower compared to India, supervisory staff, project managers and other staff positions is about 25% higher. This simply mean one thing, outsourcing in China is indeed very feasible. But then again, India and the Philippines will still be included in the picture.

Companies that Outsource: The Reasons Behind Outsourcing

Outsourcing has changed the way global business is conducted. Before, outsourcing is just a means to cut operational costs. But now, companies need to have more reasons than cutting costs to meet the additional demands of the companies. . Companies that outsource have various reasons why they do continue outsourcing. Cutting Operational Costs The main reason that companies outsource is to reduce the operational cost. According to studies, this is the primary force behind the initiative to outsource.

A company that generates quality services or products at a high cost is not welcome news at all. Therefore, good quality at lower cost comes together and the answer is to move part of its operations overseas where cheaper labor is available. Higher Retention Rates Companies that outsourced have higher customer retention rates. If a company gives much importance to combining creative programs and motivating talented agents with timely execution, then there are dramatic increases in customer retention. The company should be able to impart to there outsourcing agents that customer satisfaction is the key to customer retention. The Ability to be Flexible Outsourcing gives companies the ability to be flexible.

There are some companies that have peak and non-peak seasons. During peak seasons such as Christmas, they need more agents to work for them. Having an outsourcing partner can make hiring temporary agents easy for companies. There are several more reasons why companies turn to outsourcing aside from lower costs, higher retention rates and flexibility. Outsourcing is also a chance for companies to diversify because expertise in some areas can be found outside. Outsourcing has been discovered to be good management-wise and cost-wise. More and more companies are expected to turn into outsourcing in the future.

Negative Effects of Outsourcing

Having to deal with outside parties can also be difficult and unmanageable. As you try to outsource, you need to be cautious of the partner you would be dealing. Your business future is at stake with this partner.

To outsource is a decision that you must carefully think about. Should you decide to outsource, you should have ready at hand to identify your fundamental principles for discussion to your outsourcer, At the outset, it is necessary that relationship is harmonious and clear to both of what expectations are to be met. Unsatisfactory relationship could result to early termination of agreement or contract. One cause of failure in an outsourcing relationship is when the buyer (owner) dictates to supplier (outsourcer) of what the services and performance levels should be. The buyer lays down the expectation, the supplier process.

Another con of outsourcing is the buyer s failure to control the quality of service. The buyer awaits the finished product and hopes that they are of better quality. The buyer loses control of hiring the best-qualified people to perform the job. Outsourcer does have the tendency of hiring less qualified people to perform the job, thus reducing cost at their end.

As others see the benefits of outsourcing as reducing cost to the company, they fail to realize that productivity is lost as well. While you can invest on productivity of improving your product or service, the knowledge and skills, which are your intellectual property, are passed unto others. This allow other countries where outsourced is done to gain more skills and apply them to their other clients, which could also be a competitor of yours now or in the future. Give a careful thought about outsourcing and its effect to your business.

Why Not Outsource your Customer Service

Your customers are one of your most valuable assets in your business. Your customer s satisfaction comes first over and above anything else in the business. They make your business going and grow. A dissatisfied would either stop patronizing your product or send bad feelers to friends and family of the kind of service you provide.

Customers should be given attention and utmost care in answering to their needs. In a global competitive world, you need to be attentive to your customers needs and wants or you would eventually lose them. You certainly need more help in attending to your customers.

To solve your problem and focus more on your core business areas, you may think of having your customer service outsource. Outsourcing customer service seeks to ease out the problems you are experiencing your business. Through outsourcing your customer service, service providers are expected to handle unresolved complaints and pricing issues. They also provide suggestions as to better offers from competitors, or just simply handle your customer transaction with a personal touch. With these services, you are assured that your customers are receiving an excellent service and their complaints are handled and addressed right away.

Customer service outsourcing is can be done over the phone or through website. However, most often it is over the phone where customer concerns are received by call centers. The service provider you choose to contract with should have a unified system that will link and record your customer s historical complaints. Customers hate to start all over again about their complaints, as if they complaints are not being addressed immediately.

Give more time to focus on your business core competencies and have your customer service outsourcer handle your customer s needs.

Benefits of Data Center Outsourcing

It takes to have specialized skills to perform data entry operations and at the same time involves large amount of money to invest in computer equipments. Computer equipments have to be purchased and maintained regularly. You need highly skilled people to have them operate your data entry system.

Many companies nowadays engaged themselves to service providers involve in data entry outsourcing. It is believed to be economical and allows companies to focus on their competencies rather than worry about data center operations. For companies who are into providing reports, data center outsourcing is a big help as it fast tracks their reporting deadlines. Data center outsourcing does not need an understanding of the product, database or business. What is important is how fast, accurate and efficient the data entry is done.

Data center outsourcing manages documents as well. Service companies on data center does provide several data entry operations such as data extraction from any format, hand written, typed copy or a scanned image; and reject re-entry, data. It should also provide database maintenance at real-time data entry.

Data center outsourcing is not just about saving physical space. Some of the advantages of outsourcing data center are as follows:

1. The service operation is uninterruptible and that regular monitoring of the data can be undertaken.
2. It provides data management wherein it ensures that data have back ups

3.   There is a security measure that protects data from outside or inside hackers

4.   It provides on site trouble-shooting, and speedy response

5.   It provides a disaster recovery in case of loss in data.

Keep track of your report deadlines. Get rid of those stacks of records. Give your employees a space to breathe and move. Have your records handled; give data center outsourcing a try.

What you lose in Outsourcing

While you figure that outsourcing could solve your problems and focus more on your business core competencies, you start to realize that there is more to know about outsourcing than the benefits it could do to your business.

Outsourcing deals with your fundamental principles that of which should apply to what your contracting parties should believed in. Entering into service level agreements is just like entering into a relationship where both parties need to understand clearly, what is expected as results. If such principles do conflict, unsatisfactory relationship could possibly occur and lead to an early termination of the contract.

The following are some of the disadvantages of outsourcing:

1.   Outsourcing does damage the local labor markets. It affects the jobs of individuals within the locality as companies begin to outsource causing job disruption and employment insecurity,

2.   Outsourcing may decrease the quality or fail to realize business value. As the buyer (owner) lays his expectation and supplier (service provider) does the processing, the tendency that business value is not met. Buyer should see to it that quality service is delivered to its clients. For call centers outsourcing, linguistic features such as accents, word use and phrase used may be a problem, thus resulting to lower quality of service if call agents are having difficulty to understand the client.

3.   Higher staff turnover. As staff is trained and company skills are transferred, growing number of employees leave.

4.   Loss of control as to the hiring of qualified people to handle your product. There are unreliable suppliers who would opt

for higher profit, thus hiring or replacing qualified people with less qualified due to cost reduction.

To outsource means choosing your best partner and build trust to one another.

What Outsourcing Can Do?

How would you like to focus on your business expansion and meet new investors, leaving the nitty-gritty stuff of production to service companies to do the work. By so doing, you still continue to be the owner of your company and earn the profits, with less worry on your shoulders.

Outsourcing is the process of transfer of management or the day to day function of a business function to an outside service provider. The transfer in outsourcing involves the transfer of control. Wherein the buyer who is the owner of the company, looks for a supplier to manage the business function/ The buyer and supplier enters into a contract agreement which defines the type of service that the supplier is to deliver and the buyer s obligation to the supplier upon fulfillment of the service. The buyer is not to instruct the supplier how production is to go about, but instead communicate to the supplier the results that is expected and the process involve in accomplishing those expectations are left to the suppliers strategy.

A large number of companies have adapted outsourcing and found to be a strategic management option. In a competitive world, businesses should start to focus on their core competencies. While it has been criticized to cause unemployment to some countries and is threat to the economy, outsourcing has positive effects on a large level. Through outsourcing, companies can pass the product to its consumers at reduced costs, as there will be high demand for the product if sold at a price lower than what your competitors are selling. The products are marketed as a high tech product due to the high quality control placed into it.

What Covers Engineering Outsourcing

To reduce the headcount of people in an organization is essential if the business is modeled to focus on its core competencies and swing away from hands on engineering. Engineering outsourcing does not mean getting rid of the business engineers but limiting outsourcing to non essential jobs and retaining your talented engineers in coming up of new innovations for the firm.

Engineering outsourcing are those transactional functions that are repetitive in nature and involves writing skills. Having to engineer outsource is to allow a company to focus on project management, process engineering and technology integration. One of the reasons as well is to fill in gaps of expertise and be able to meet fast track schedules.

Engineering Outsourcing calls for services that include aerospace design, construction, pharmaceuticals, automotive design and industrial machinery products. As customers become demanding, companies would have to compete with each other to win customer s satisfaction.

To outsource engineering services, the company should see to it that the outsourcer could provide high quality engineering services and its employees are highly qualified professionals to perform the work. Some of the engineering services should have specialization in the field of Structural, Mechanical & Electronic Engineering - analysis and design, embedded software, Plant Design, Process Engineering, Plant Automation Services and Enterprise Asset Management and OEM solutions.

Engineering outsourcing is acquiring a momentum, in as much as it deals with labor-intensive engineering processes (structural drafting and detailing, conversion services, cost estimations and a lot more). It assures businesses of a quick turnaround time, good price competition, and its ability to customize the software based on the project management itself.

Effects of Global Outsourcing

While some have looked into outsourcing as a threat to a country s economy and individuals fear the loss of their job as a company do outsource, most find global outsourcing as beneficial to the international market. Global outsourcing assist in the creation of newer international markets, global citizenship, and the recognition of global talent and in a wider scope helps in the economic development of all participating countries. Not all are aware but global outsourcing is aim to create better jobs in the future. The following are top ten reasons why companies do outsourcing:

1. Operational costs are reduced and controlled.
2. Enable companies to focus on strategic plan.
3. Allow accessibility to world-class capabilities.
4. Free company from internal resources and focus on other purposes.
5. Allow accessibility to resources that are not available internally.
6. Increased reengineering benefits.
7. Ability to handle difficult functions or out of control tasks.

In a highly global competitive world, companies and service providers should be aware of the growing service markets including the needs of its customers. Global outsourcing allows companies to choose among service providers as to the best service would suit and would carry the job well. It is important that business carefully scrutinized the capabilities of these service providers. The demand for global outsourcing is increasing and there are several providers for businesses to choose.

Government Has Gone Outsourcing

Government agencies have started to outsource services from the private sector in order to keep a fast track of accomplishing their objectives towards helping the country s economy and security needs. Though some find it very hard to negotiate with the public sector as the process of selection is so bureaucratic and tedious, the government sector has learned to expedite the selection of vendors to serve their needs.

One of the factors that led government to outsource services is to increase its focus on privatization, e-government initiatives, difficulties in attracting and retaining skilled staff, the growing emphasis in interagency collaboration, and pressure to improve financial performance. Government agencies can earn its rewards by deciding to work with IT service vendors to speed up its work output.

Three factors why government decided to outsource IT service:

1. Cost. Government agencies are not knowledgeable enough of having control into the costs of current operation. They are aware of what they are spending but they do not always know where the money goes. Outsourcing is a tool to resolve agencies cost dilemma as service providers gives its agencies a chance to understand how business is to operate. There is a clear understanding of the relationship between the costs and benefits of IT. 2.

Technology. Government agencies technology problems on their inability to keep paced with e-government initiatives, demands for greater interagency collaboration, and the need for standardized environments. Government agencies still work on outdated equipment.

3.   Personnel. Government agencies aging workforce and the non-IT staff.

Government Outsourcing is an answer to having the delivery of better service to taxpayers on time, after all taxpayers deserve to see results on where their money is used.

Getting Health Service You Need

Your employees are one of your most valuable assets in the company. It is your responsibility to ensure that they are healthy and well balanced as they report to work. Unhealthy and a unbalanced employee has the tendency of being unproductive and this adds up to the company costs. Companies should see to it that its employees are taken care and protected. For this reason, companies instead of hiring a medical team, seek for a healthcare service that will cater to the needs of the company s employees. This is called as healthcare outsourcing, where employees are sent to healthcare service providers to ensure that their health are being handled well.

Like all other businesses, the healthcare companies have started its way of outsourcing its services as well. Healthcare companies have been outsourcing tasks such as environmental services, nutrition services, clinical functions, information technology etc.

Hospitals and other small healthcare companies cannot afford a wide range of medical professionals especially when there are no patients to attend to all the time. The healthcare outsourcing provides a chance for healthcare companies to refer to medical professionals on a as need basis without indefinite commitment.

The healthcare outsourcing gave rise also to the many administrative difficulties in the area of the preparation of insurance policy procedures and dealing with complicated claim forms. These types of healthcare outsource deals with medical billing. In this situation, healthcare outsourcers would have to hire billing professionals. These professionals would act as consultants for doctors and assist patients in dealing all medical billing needs. Another form of healthcare outsourcing is through medical transcription. This process involves converting into standard text the dictated information provided by doctor s to the patient s medical record.

Healthcare Outsourcing , the efficient way of giving your health utmost priority.

The Difference that HR Outsourcing Makes to Your Company

Human resources is one of the key components in business operations. However, there are times wherein many businesses focus more on other issues that they don t find enough time in managing human resources functions. There is no other way to deal on this dilemma other than resorting to outsourcing. Human resources outsourcing is the answer in finding a more cost-effective approach instead of hiring an in-house human resources staff.

HR firms nowadays offer a wide-variety of service solutions to companies that need to establish their core business objectives while at the same time, establishing and maintaining good HR policies. There are a few questions that need to be answered before hiring an HR firm. First, is it just fine for the company to let someone else handle their HR functions? Second, does the business currently have adequate HR resources to manage their HR needs? Lastly, can the company afford to pay an HR outsourcing firm? Once all the answers to these questions were carefully evaluated and the results lean towards HR outsourcing, then this could just be the right thing to do for the company.

Choosing which among HR firms that will best suit the company s needs is the next step. There are a lot of things to consider, and cost is the primarily the deciding factor. These include general HR experience, its expertise in the industry and range of outsourcing services it provides. In addition, a good HR outsourcing firm possesses three things:
(a) understanding of company priorities,
(b) its available resources and

(c) flexibility of its contract. Keeping this in mind will make the transition to getting an HR firm easier for the company to handle.

Less worry, Human Resource Outsourcing is the Key

Management of people is difficult. Handling difficult people is stressful. Running a business is even harder as you tend to reach for your main objective of earning profit. With all these coming your way, you need high-qualified people to perform some tasks as you attend to the core competencies of your business.

Major businesses are outsourcing their human resource. The following human resources outsource services offered are

- Payroll administration. This includes the preparation of checks, handling of taxes and recording of sick time and vacation time: Produce checks, handle taxes, and deal with sick time and vacation time,

- Employee benefits. This includes Health, Medical, Life, 401(k) plans, cafeteria plans, etc.

- HR management. This involves the recruiting, hiring, and firing. This type of service does the background interviews, exit interviews, and wage reviews.

- Risk management. This service deals with workers' compensation, dispute resolution, safety inspection, office policies and handbooks.

Human Resource outsourcing would support your business necessary towards growth in the business industry. While you worry of how to expand your business, outsourcing human resource takes care of how things are to be handled in your workplace. They see to it that human resource are taken care of and are paid on time. Human Resource Outsourcing aim is to streamline processes and make things clear to employees.

Cost would be the deciding factor in selecting the human resource service provider. It is important that both parties should have compatibility of work ethics. It is required that service providers are well experienced in handling human resource necessary to carry out the job.

Human Resources Outsourcing- How Does it Work?

Human resources outsourcing is a smart management practice that many companies have to take advantage of. Embracing the concept of such outsourcing option is very compelling and at the same time, essential in providing excellent service to the needs of any company. Such advantages include:

(a) more productive use of time and company resources;

(b) improved business focus; and

(c) expert guidance coming from across the business spectrum.

An HR firm is an extension of company culture. This is the reason why there is a need to find one that fits the company s image. But then again, it is not always necessary to let a firm handle all HR functions for the company. This usually happens when confidential information is at stake that may result to breach of company security. There are also some companies that are not that confident in handing off all HR responsibilities to one particular firm, thus only outsourcing HR tasks that are often labor intensive and time consuming.

Say for example, a company is in need of IT professionals. Services of an HR firm can then be acquired to search for qualified candidates. Once an applicant passes the minimum qualifications, the HR firm will then report this to the company, give assessments and provide warranted recommendations. However, final selection will be done by the company s hiring panel. There are other specialized services that HR firms provide and these include the development of employee handbook, establishment of performance management metrics and setting up of compensation packages.

This is basically how the process works for human resources outsourcing. Either all or selective, HR outsourcing definitely provides convenience to a company in its finest form.

Outsourcing in India   A Trade Secret

India remains as one of the top Business Process Outsourcing (BPO) providers, not only dominating the whole of Asia but the rest of the planet as well. Profits keep on coming and the Indian BPO industry continues to grow that it even emerge as one of the key investment markets in this side of the world today. In 2005 alone, there were over 400 companies operating within the Indian BPO space, and these include third-party service providers and captive units (of both Indian and Multinational Corporations). India is ideal for BPO primarily due to cheaper bandwidth, which leads to low telecom costs for leased lines. To top it all, India has a competitive English-speaking workforce provided with accent reduction training classes to improve more on communication and interaction skills.

India s dominance in the BPO industry started in the early 1980 s when European airlines, such as British Airways, have started using Delhi as the location for back-office operations. On the second half, American Express also strengthened its back-office operations in New Delhi. In the 1990 s, General Electric (GE) formed an enterprise called GECIS (GE Capital International Services) and it became a huge success that GE even ramp up their Indian workforce. It was during 2000 when third party BPOs came into the picture and one of the early BPOs established is Spectramind. In 2002, Wipro bought Spectramind and by then, BPO had become conventional just like India s IT industry. The BPO industry grew rapidly that it reached as high as 38% on 2005. Among approximately one million workers, some 40% appears to be directly working in the BPO and IT sector. This is such an achievement on today s Indian BPO industry.

Indian Outsourcing: More Savings at Par Excellence

Indian outsourcing has been a popular choice for offshore outsourcing. Businesses are always looking for ways to cut costs and so they would tend to go to developing countries when they decide to outsource.

Indian outsourcing has been an obvious choice for many because not only is labor in India cheaper, the country also has an advantage over other developing countries when it comes to technology. Its citizens are also educated and most Indians also know how to speak and write English well so businesses in the US and in UK don t have to worry about the quality of the service. Indian outsourcing can perform at par excellence with outsourcing in their countries.

Businesses still get the same benefits from hiring an outsourcing company from the US. Indian outsourcing would definitely give them more time for income generating activities. With better and innovative products and services, they will be able to make and keep their clients happy. Their company will be able to gain more market share. And in addition to that, savings just run higher. Because labor is relatively cheaper in India the cost for outsourcing is lower too. They also save in office capital investment and in office inventory. Indian outsourcing companies are up to date when it comes to technology and industry practices too so US companies and those from the UK really can outsource with confidence.

With these advantages companies get from Indian outsourcing, more and more companies are bound to outsource offshore.

Indian outsourcing, on its part, would tend to grow not only in scope and in market share but in quality and competitiveness too.

Information Technology Outsourcing: Gaining IT Expertise with Less Investment

Information technology outsourcing is one area that has been gaining more and more popularity in most business industries. Information technology has a broad scope and every company would have a special need for their business. Because our world is now technology-based, one cannot do away with information technology. In fact, companies have now become more and more IT dependent.

Having one company s own IT personnel requires employment of especially skilled personnel. If the company doesn t have the technical knowhow to begin with, it will not be equipped to hire the best people for the company. Also, having IT employees usually means paying high salaries. The company can then turn to information technology outsourcing instead. Information technology outsourcing companies can provide them solutions that are appropriate to company needs. They will also provide the company with the expertise. What s even better is that outsourcing their IT would usually cost lesser. Not only will they save on hiring costs they would not have to train IT employees too. IT outsourcing companies have well trained and updated systems and personnel. So whether the company needs is web hosting, e-commerce, web security and solutions or website design and administration, IT outsourcing companies have the answer to their problems and needs.

With IT functioning well and smoothly, the company can go on doing what they can to improve company performance. They will be able to engage in product and service research and development. And they will be able to serve their customers better. With better IT systems, innovative products and services and happy customers, the company will gain a lot from information technology outsourcing.

Infrastructure Outsourcing: Providing the Company with a Solid Backbone

In today s competitive world, businesses have turned to infrastructure outsourcing not only as a cost cutting option but also as a part of their strategy for fast delivery and better remote and on site management. They have found infrastructure outsourcing to be beneficial in providing them with the right solutions and helping them achieve high company performance.

Since IT is important in running the company nowadays, having a good IT backbone is really important. The company must bear in mind that in order to have a company that is operating at high performance they would need the appropriate infrastructure. Running and maintaining it should be cost effective as well.

Through infrastructure outsourcing, the company gains the expertise of the company they are contracting with. With the right knowhow, they are able to put in place the appropriate IT systems and applications to run the company quite smoothly and to bring company made products to its customers as well. New technologies are also implemented more smoothly. So when transformation is deemed necessary it is done with less hassle and less disruption in operations.

With the right infrastructure in place, the company will be able to trim down costs and operate in an optimal way. Company information can also easily be collated and turned in to company executives and managers to aid them in decision making. With easy data capture, areas for improvement can easily be identified and dealt with. So infrastructure outsourcing actually provides the company a holistic assistance. It s not just savings it brings but it also helps the company operate in an easier and in a more efficient way.

International Outsourcing Equals Less Labor Costs and Better Company Performance

International outsourcing has been an increasing trend. Businesses not only have gone to outsourcing but they are outsourcing several company tasks offshore. Businesses have looked into hiring labor from third world countries such as India, Philippines, China, Mexico, Israel, Brazil and Malaysia. The reason why businesses in developed countries like the US and UK have done this is that labor from these countries are cheaper than in their country. Their companies then are able to operate in a more optimal manner. Because they are in effect operating in a more cost effective way, they have greater chances of achieving greater income and growth.

By outsourcing some minor tasks, the company is able direct more attention to its core competencies. The outsourced tasks are done by these international outsourcing companies so there are fewer tasks for the company to do. With fewer employees, the company is also able to save on hiring, training, office inventory and office space. International outsourcing companies update and train their own employees at their own costs too so this even gives the company additional savings and quality of service.

And just like any other outsourcing company, international outsourcing companies usually have a strict turn-around time to follow. The company can rely on their good and accommodating service. Outputs are usually delivered on time too. With reports or whatever output available when they are needed, the company will be able to operate smoothly and more efficiently.

Some may have concerns over the fact that work is done across the globe. However, that should not be a barrier for them. The technology of today affords companies the luxury to outsource offshore. They just have to pick the international outsourcing company that they know they can trust and they can expect to receive good service from.

Keeping Up with IT Outsourcing

If you are considering a future career in IT or, you are currently working as an IT professional in the US, chances are you may have already encountered the term IT outsourcing . Yes, this term is not relatively new as it is obviously one of the reasons why jobs are being transferred to offshore firms based in India or the rest of Asia. The primary reason is that these firms operate in low costs with a considerably same level of knowledge, skills and competencies. If this is the case, does this mean that the IT industry in the US is almost reaching its endpoint?

The answer is a big NO of course as this is pretty much too early to tell. Though quite alarming, a profession in the IT industry in the US is still promising like in the previous years it offers good pay, numerous opportunities and long term job stability. But then again, since IT outsourcing is somehow getting ahead of the competition, IT professionals in the US can still do something to cope with this situation. Here are some tips to consider:

(a)   Panic is not an option. If you are currently an IT student, do not question yourself if indeed you landed on the right course. Just do the most out of what you can get.
(b)   Accept reality. IT outsourcing is here to stay, maybe within a couple of years or so. Stay focus and strategize by being an IT generalist.
(c)   Start your own business and think of out-of-the-box ideas. New big market opportunities will soon emerge and you have to be prepared for it.

Above all, do not be afraid of changing IT market trends. Even with competition around, be on top of your game and everything will false into place.

Job Outsourcing Practices Continues to Grow As Many Realize Its Benefits

Job outsourcing is a very common practice nowadays. It is so perhaps because businesses have found it to be more cost efficient and less demanding on their daily operations. All they have to do is dish out the jobs to be done and they come back in finished output.

Job outsourcing can range from jobs like accounting, research telemarketing to information technology related jobs. More and more companies have just found it to be beneficial that others have tried to outsource what they can. They have resorted to outsource the non-core activities of the company in order to give way to product and service development and company building.

Job outsourcing have been found to be cost efficient for most companies trying this strategy. They were able to operate with fewer personnel. Because of this they needed to do less hiring. Training activities were limited to their employees who were doing core activities too. And yet they still get the same or maybe even better service when they outsource certain tasks.

Job outsourcing companies usually have expertise in their field. They are also updated in new practices and new tools. They are more service proactive too. The turn-around time would normally be shorter and companies generally deliver finished projects and tasks on time. And because outsourcing is now a very competitive market companies providing them really try to deliver the best service and they offer them at competitive prices as well. While more and more companies arise, services are also getting better and better.

Legal Outsourcing:Taking Care of Legal Matters in a Cost Effective Way

Legal outsourcing has been to answer for smaller firms legal needs. Since they have insufficient budget for hiring in house lawyers that have enough experience and expertise in areas that they need lawyers for, they have opted to outsource their legal needs instead. Even larger companies have at times turned to legal outsourcing on instances where their in-house lawyers lack the expertise on the problem at hand.

Legal outsourcing can either be a one time or a continuous service rendering. The latter would definitely free company officials to concentrate in their money making activities rather than worrying about legal matters. Legal aspects of the business cannot just be disregarded if the company wants to continue doing business. That s why they would need to go for legal outsourcing.

There are several legal services legal outsourcing companies offer. Some of them are drafting procedures, giving assistance to regulatory inspections and making sure that the whole company is complying with company policies and that they are also in compliance with regulations. Others would also extend a hand in drafting and negotiating company contracts. Other services include conducting special reviews, serving as consultants to top management on legal matters and reputational risks, setting up and documenting hedge funds and engaging in due diligence. All of these are quite a handful for a company executive to look into one by one. But with that responsibility taken away, that person and the rest of the company will be able concentrate on improving their products and services. They will also be able to save on legal costs. As a result, legal outsourcing helps the company to operate in an efficient and a productive way.

Manufacturing Outsourcing Is the Key to Competitive Finished Products

Many companies in some industries would need parts or perhaps even ingredients in order to come up with their finished products. Some companies opt to manufacture these parts in their own plants. However, many companies have found that this is not cost effective. That s why they turn to manufacturing outsourcing. They are better off ordering these parts from other companies than making them themselves. When they do this they will have more time to allocate on improving and maintaining the quality and competitiveness of their products.

But then getting a manufacturing company to partner with is not very easy. The company must find the manufacturing outsourcing company that will be able to produce what they need with the level of quality they require. So before they contract with another company to produce some products for them they should define the specifications and the quality test they want to be performed. They should also tell them the schedule they want followed. And lastly, the two companies must agree on the price that will be beneficial to both companies.

Quality is usually a great consideration. The company should be careful on checking the products that they are getting. If they outsource below par parts, then they would end up producing products that are of poor quality too. Getting the products on time is also important. If they don t arrive on schedule, manufacturing in the company s own plants will be disrupted because of lack of materials. And of course, they should be getting the products at cost effective prices. This is important so they will be able to offer their products at competitive prices too.

Medical Outsourcing: When Medical Costs Are High And Quality Is Required

The cost of medical care in the US has continuously increased in the recent years. More and more citizens are unable to afford expensive medical care when they need it. Some even have chosen to forego such service in order to avoid such high costs.

Medical outsourcing has been given as a solution for the reducing medical care cost while still maintaining the quality of medical care service every citizen deserves. Medical outsourcing actually means going to another country to obtain medical attention for non-emergency diseases. While there are some that are concerned with quality of medical care service one would get in a foreign land compared to the one he would get at home, researches have proven that the level of quality that people with medical outsourcing plans get are actually at par if not better than what they have at home.

Many people have come to realize this. In fact, there are more and more Americans who are going to other countries to get medical attention. And a large number of these people getting medical outsourcing plans belong to the middle class and the upper class. Most of them have done so either or both to get specialized medical treatment and to get lower cost medical care services.

Because of the disparity in cost, even employers have started to look into medical outsourcing as a possible solution to the problem of high medical cost in the US. Companies have started to implement this policy in providing medical benefits to their employees in order to lower cost and in effect, operate the company in a more cost effective way.

Oasis Outsourcing: The Answer to Employee Administration Burden

Oasis Outsourcing is the world s leading professional employer organization. It caters to services related to human resources. What Oasis offers are human resources services such as worker insurances, worker compensation, recruitment services, unemployment insurance, 401 plans and risk management.

Oasis Outsourcing gives a new meaning to employee relations. Being a professional employer organization, it helps employers or companies manage employee services. Human resource administration can be done easily. The company is assured that their employees will be paid their salaries on time and they will receive benefits that satisfy federal and state law requirements.

Oasis Outsourcing will provide cost effective and appropriate employee related solutions. It will make administrative functions less complicated and less of a problem. With Oasis Outsourcing, everything can be taken care of from recruitment and payroll to employee benefits and insurance.

And because Oasis also helps companies with risk management, the company can implement a safe working place policy. While Oasis is helping them in managing their responsibilities to their employees, it even extends their service up to creating and ensuring the safety of their employees while at work. They do so by conducting regular inspections on the work place. From the inspections, Oasis will recommend safety protocols. And then they will also help management ensure a drug-free workplace.

In effect, when the company partners with Oasis it shares with it their employee responsibilities. The company remains in control of employee duty delegation while Oasis takes care of the other half. Oasis takes care of employee salary and benefits. With administration done by their other half, the company can now get their heads focused on the propagation of their products and their company. They are able to operate better and in a least expensive way.

Offshore Outsourcing   Is Your Company Ready?

The true essence of offshore outsourcing is just very simple. When a company hires another company to perform business functions in a country other than where the products or services are being developed or manufactured, then that is offshore outsourcing. Since most of the work is being done outside, this makes the labor force of established countries such as the US and the UK highly vulnerable. This issue has been the discussion of a lot of debates and conferences, but still offshore outsourcing dominates the industry as it presents a lot of advantages in terms of cost and benefits.

Some of the work that is being outsourced to countries such as the Philippines, India and China include customer support, computer programming, and data entry. There are even some companies that acquire the services of third-party companies to do critical business functions such as payroll, accounting, and human resource services. These functions were further categorized into four as the basic types of offshore outsourcing. These are:
(a) ITO or Information Technology Outsourcing   all about IT services,
(b) BPO or Business Process Outsourcing   call center management, insurance processing claims etc.,
(c) Software R & D   software development done offshore and
(d) KPO or Knowledge Process Outsourcing   higher skill sets such as reading X-rays, handling accounting functions, performing investment researches etc.

As mentioned, the driving force that makes offshore outsourcing the newest trend in doing business is always due to low costs. If work is easy to set up, repeatable, has high information content and can be transmitted over the internet, then the company is more than ready to resort to offshore outsourcing.

The Basic of Outsourcing: The Process of Getting an Outsource Supplier

Outsourcing services to a third-party company is such a crucial decision that should be approved by the company s business owners, the board and its management. This process usually takes weeks or even months to accomplish, starting with the identification of what services are to be outsourced. After that, there is a need to build a business case to justify this decision. Once everything was put on paper and signed by the key people in the organization, then the search for the outsourcing partner will take place. The company (client) then will be issuing Request for Proposal (RFP) to shortlist suppliers and determine their proposal plus price.

The next step is the process of elimination, with the client evaluating the proposal of each supplier. This also involves a lot of face-to-face board meetings to clarify certain terms and conditions while getting the supplier s response. The client will then cut the list and only the ones qualified will remain. This process is also known as down select . Eventually, this will lead to the due diligence stage wherein two suppliers remain to maintain the competition. The supplier that submits the best and final offer will obviously be the one selected. The client and the chosen supplier will then go into competitive negotiations and convert these into contractual agreement.

The contractual agreement is considered the heart of the outsourcing deal, defining how the client and supplier will work together. This document contains the terms and conditions of the contract among other particulars that are necessary before the actual signing occurs. Once everything is settled, transition of services will then take place. This marks the end of the outsourcing process and the start of a client-supplier relationship.

Outsourcing Accounting Keeps a Company Lean and Efficient

Accounting is an important part of the business. But there are yet more important things the company should concentrate on like how they could improve their products, what product innovation is needed and how they could build their customer base. That s why many companies now have opted to outsource accounting.

When they outsource accounting, companies are bound to realize huge savings on operating expenses. They will have fewer employees to hire so they will have less to train as well. They would need less office equipment, office space and office inventory. All of these often translate up to a 50% savings on their operations.

Outsourcing accounting companies are generally composed of high caliber individuals so the company can expect accurate accounting. Hiring them actually gives them the same expertise they would have had they hired their own accountants. But the good thing is that they would have to pay less. Outsourcing accounting companies are also usually updated to new technology, new practices and new tools. So the company also gets the advantages from these.

Another thing is that outsourcing accounting firms would tend to be customer oriented. The company can expect to receive reports on time and they can also request them as needed. These firms know that they should be service oriented too. In effect, they can even be more effective than having an in house accounting group. Company executives and managers will have the necessary reports in order to make better judgment. And with the peace of mind that accounting reports would be ready when needed, they can now concentrate on more important activities like income generation, product development and customer satisfaction. The company will be able to grow and they will be able to operate in the most optimal way.

Offshore Outsourced Call Centers: How the Philippines Benefits from this Business

From among the developing countries tapped for labor force for outsourcing, the Philippines is in the top list. There is no doubt how call center business contributes to this country s increased employment rate and an essential increase in overall income.

There are over than 100 call centers established within various locations in the Philippines. Such emerging outsourcing business provides Filipinos with high-paying job opportunities. Somehow it provides opportunities among fresh graduates or unemployed citizens who may be having difficulty finding niche or jobs in their respective fields.

Philippine offshore outsourced call center providers mainly serve various numbers of U.S. companies, which are increasing in number over time. For a location-based service like an outbound call handling services, these call centers provide support to different business areas, such as telemarketing, sales confirmation, account reinstatement or reactivation, credit and collection, and other more customer support services. On the other hand, inbound call servicing includes technical support, customer service or product inquiries, customer requests and/or complaints, sales, and billings.

The nation s culture and loyalty among Filipino workers would be the factors to why the call center industry is increasingly attractive in the global market. Historically, Filipinos have long dealt with various cultures, particularly those that have once colonized the country for several decades. These events have somehow given Filipinos abilities and competencies to interact and relate to different cultures. In addition, having relatives from abroad also contributes to familiarity with American language, culture, and lifestyle. In contrast, loyalty may perhaps be considered an innate characteristic among Filipinos. Filipino workers tend to stay longer and committed to their work, which consequently what attracts call center business opportunities in the country. The Philippines indeed benefit from this business and perhaps will continue to.

The Basic of Outsourcing: The Process of Getting an Outsource Supplier

Outsourcing services to a third-party company is such a crucial decision that should be approved by the company s business owners, the board and its management. This process usually takes weeks or even months to accomplish, starting with the identification of what services are to be outsourced. After that, there is a need to build a business case to justify this decision. Once everything was put on paper and signed by the key people in the organization, then the search for the outsourcing partner will take place. The company (client) then will be issuing Request for Proposal (RFP) to shortlist suppliers and determine their proposal plus price.

The next step is the process of elimination, with the client evaluating the proposal of each supplier. This also involves a lot of face-to-face board meetings to clarify certain terms and conditions while getting the supplier s response. The client will then cut the list and only the ones qualified will remain. This process is also known as down select . Eventually, this will lead to the due diligence stage wherein two suppliers remain to maintain the competition. The supplier that submits the best and final offer will obviously be the one selected. The client and the chosen supplier will then go into competitive negotiations and convert these into contractual agreement.

The contractual agreement is considered the heart of the outsourcing deal, defining how the client and supplier will work together. This document contains the terms and conditions of the contract among other particulars that are necessary before the actual signing occurs. Once everything is settled, transition of services will then take place. This marks the end of the outsourcing process and the start of a client-supplier relationship.

India s global plea: Stop Outsourced Jobs in India

Americans are not the only ones adversely affected by implications of outsourcing. Surprisingly, India has expressed its voice for America to stop this new workforce system, specifically outsourcing call centers that handle customer support. India is among the developing countries globally known for its outsourced service to first world countries, such as America and in Europe.

Over the years, India has gained optimistic reputation for its outsourcing call centers. They have created a skilled workforce that can fluently speak in English. And although India recognizes the benefits and advantages of outsourcing in the global market, but how it begins to cost their society depressingly results to more apprehensions and forthcoming thoughts as how outsourcing can completely change their societal norms and systems.

Indian skilled workers were trained so vigorously to speak American over the telephone that unconsciously and substantially they have become Americans. Indian community cannot help but to regard them as American immigrants resulting to a distinct pressure in their community, which consequently causes some structural changes in their society. Learned American attitudes, behaviors, and preferences are becoming more and more visible among this trained skilled Americanized outsourced workforce. They have become overly confident and reacting to almost everything and anything, becoming forthright in their words and actions in a community wherein respect and warmth are highly valued and preserved. Foreign products are increasingly patronized, their lifestyle eventually practiced. Such events seemingly manifest how influential and persuading first world countries can be, even to point of letting go of one s cultural heritage to embrace a new one.

Until now, Indians remain firm to their stand against outsourced jobs, and are doing their best to stop further changes this emerging workforce system may cause to their community, both their culture and economy.

Outsourced Information Technology: Benefits and Advantages

Information Technology (IT) is as meticulous as in the other internal core functions (e.g., payroll, sales and marketing, bookkeeping) that a company would have. Thus, seeking for the best outsource IT provider will certainly work mainly for the company s gain.

Following are some basic reasons why outsourcing IT functions is a beneficial decision for maintaining an IT department rather than administering it internally.

Outsourcing IT functions provides the company the advantage to gaining more control over its IT-related costs. The company benefits from an extensive expertise that is being provided by outsource IT experts at a reasonable cost. Also, the company only needs to pay whenever specific IT services are needed and met.

Furthermore, the company achieves gains with regard to staffing benefits and the quality of service the outsourced provider manages. Specifically, turning to an outsourced provider gives the company an assurance that the jobs contracted are managed and carried out by guaranteed skilled IT consultants or experts. Outsource staff can provide quality service and performance, resulting to a fulfilling support to their principal company. Basically, an outsourced provider is paid for completion of services or jobs contracted to them.

Surely, a company would also want to deal only with a competent outsource provider, to establish an agreement with IT professionals who can also be skilled with the latest IT software and technology. IT outsourced providers will have to use standardized software and equipment, which results to saving more resources while quality good and/or services are provided.

What is mostly benefitting for the company however, is passing on its IT core functions to a selected IT outsourced providers. In this way the company can focus more on its core business and improving competencies while the non-priority functions are handled by respective outsourced provider.

Understanding the Need to Outsource Jobs

Outsourcing increasingly gains recognition and importance to various companies, both locally and globally. It is even sought as an alternative and efficient approach to reducing workload and resource pressures by companies or corporations of various ranges, such as large manufacturing and business corporations, medium- and small-sized business corporations, and even some private and small companies.

Company functions or jobs that are commonly outsourced include: book keeping and financial services, business consulting, human resources services, internal marketing, medical billing, proofreading and editing, transcription, writing and translation, data entry, DTP/typesetting, handwriting services, legal services, animation and multimedia, software and technology, web design and development, and computer-aided design (CAD) and/or com- puter-aided manufacturing (CAM).

Outsourcing enable companies to save significant amount of resources such as money and time since jobs get done and services are paid at lower cost. Moreover, they are even able to gain access to more potential workforce and further positive projections.

Companies however, have some important things to consider before getting themselves into outsourcing. First, they must come up with a master list detailing which in-house activities are needed to be outsourced, and then ranked them by priority. Second, com- panies must carefully assess and choose which outsourcing compa- nies they plan to engage with. Similar to hiring a regular/full-time or part-time worker, evaluation on the outsource provider s work and experience profile will be helpful to make sure that expectations are guaranteed. Lastly, companies still have to maintain management over the outsourced jobs or services. Assigning an in-house assistant to supervise outsource providers assures that desired level of output are achieved.

Generally, outsourcing provides an alternative solution, particularly for companies that strive for competitiveness, allowing them to focus more on immediate and important fundamental tasks and issues, while other particulars are handled by the outsource providers.

Some Benefits from an Outsourced Payroll Provider

Outsourcing payroll can be an easy solution for a growing and thriving company. This specialized outsource service helps the company from using its resources to accomplishing certain meticulous tasks rather than concentrating more on managing and improving its core business efforts.

Payroll management is a tedious work as it requires a significant amount of time and absolute focus to achieve accuracy. It involves precise keeping and updating of records, includes calculating and paying payroll taxes, and corresponding well with current personnel. An outsource payroll provider can be useful as an efficient and cost-effective solution.

Generally there are eight noted benefits from outsourcing payroll.

First, it avoids unnecessary penalties since outsourced payroll providers take on inclusive responsibilities in processing, calculating, and preparing payrolls; and in submitting monthly or quarterly tax-related reports all on time.

Secondly, it reduces costs since internal payroll management requires more costs than having the task itself outsourced to a payroll provider.

Third, it lessens the pain of getting too preoccupied and overwhelmed by merely doing such meticulous job.

Fourth, it offers direct-to-deposit account option, which only possible when working with a payroll provider eliminating the hassles of paperwork and all.

Fifth, it saves time allowing the company more free in indulging to productive and income-generating activities or projects.

Sixth, it avoids getting headache from opting to often complicated and time-consuming payroll management-related software or technology.

Seven, it provides a company to make the most of the external payroll expertise with regard to regularly changing regulations, government forms, and tax rates.

Lastly, it reduces possible business risk such as career movements among employees or changes in staff structure.

For a company to remain focused on matters important for its growth and accomplishments, a beneficial and efficient payroll provider can be helpful.

Gaining More from an Outsourced Sales Provider

Similar with the other outsource service providers, outsourcing sales can be an optimistic solution for a thriving, and expanding company. Basically, this progressively recognized service enables a company to use and focus its internal resources more on added-value and income-generating endeavors, such as producing a new product or service, developing strategies when the company begins its venture for business expansion, or for the company to simply succeed in improving and innovating its core competencies and expertise.

Outsourced sales provider can decrease a company s functional costs. It also provides immediate access to competent sales and marketing force, experts who may not be otherwise accessible.

Further reasons as why a company must seek service from outsource provider for its sale, are as follows. First is the pay per sale basis, which means that outsource provider will not be paid unless there is selling of products. This reduces the risk of needing to pay for salary and benefits. Second is the guaranteed expertise that the outsource providers can provide.

The company is ensured that hired outsource providers have the required expertise or experience specifically in selling products. Therefore, whether they are reps, distributors, agents, wholesalers, and so forth, what is important is they know how to make sales. Thirdly, is picking the competent outsource providers based on specialization, preferably in markets and industries. Fourth, is the great possibility of establishing an instant and therefore securing a long-term relationship between the company and outsource provider. Such relationship builds up credibility and results to an increase product movement in the market. Lastly, is opening further opportunities for the company s products, which definitely results to a better sales function.

A company can only do so much. Outsourcing sales function ensures an enhanced and innovative selling and promotion of products.

Why Companies Worldwide Outsource To India

Over the years of providing various outsource services globally, India has gained superiority when it comes to outsourcing specific core functions or services. Such event led for India to be recognized as the global outsourcing solution particularly in the fields of software development and technology, as well as software-enabled services.

Other services or functions, which can be outsourced to India, may be categorized under IT and software services and IT-enabled services. Examples of IT and software services include product development, software testing, data entry, and programming to name a few.

IT-enabled services, on the other hand, include business process outsourcing or BPO (e.g., customer relationship management), back-office operations (e.g., accounting, payroll), web development services (e.g., portals, e-commerce), infrastructures (e.g., communication and messaging, e-business operations), communications and networking (e.g., telecommunications, computer telephony), media and entertainment (e.g., animation, film-making), call centers (e.g., helpdesk, bookkeeping services), operations (e.g., web applications, e-marketplaces), relationship management (e.g. customer care service), community management (e.g., opening e-business channels), medical transcription (e.g., clinical notes), and on-site services (e.g., on-site assistance, software installation).

Outsourcing to India provides companies worldwide with a cost-effective solution. Getting the contracted services done at affordable costs without the need to hire regular staff and need for the companies to pay for salaries and benefits. Premium quality of services is produced and received since the companies are guaranteed with skilled expertise and credibility of outsourced providers in India. Apparently, the outsourcing helps in reducing some operating costs since these service providers are paid once services or deliverables are completed, which is usually inclusive in the agreed upon sub-contract agreement.

Last and most importantly, the companies are able to optimize their time and use company resources to concentrate more in improving their core competencies and developing profit-generating projects.

Presenting the Various Benefits of Outsourcing

Greater returns, bigger rewards this is what outsourcing is all about. But how can one company maximize all the benefits that outsourcing provides? The first step is always choosing the best outsourcing firm that can be your company s lifetime partner on your ticket to success. Once everything is set up, immediate return-on-investment (ROI) awaits your company. Some of the valuable outsourcing benefits include the following:

(a)   Cost Savings   One of the primary reasons why companies resort to outsourcing is for the purpose of lowering production costs. Since most of the services rendered offshore such as in China, India and the Philippines are way cheaper than in the Western world, companies are taking advantage of outsourcing and still get almost the same value in terms of quality and performance.

(b)   Knowledge and Competencies   Every person working for a firm that takes good care of the outsourcing needs of large (and even small) companies are equally trained and competent to carry out business functions that will definitely result to total customer satisfaction.

(c)   Capacity Management   Outsourcing gives the company specific tools to manage production capacity or business output in a more flexible manner.

(d)   Appropriate Staffing   There are a lot of knowledgeable and skillful people around and most of them work in outsourcing firms. Your company will not definitely run out of talented people to man the job by getting the most out of outsourcing.

Indeed, outsourcing promises a lot of benefits to companies. However, it would be best to put all expectations down on a piece of paper that will be signed by both parties to gain better understanding of the partnership. This will eventually eliminate conflicts in the future as both will be committed in achieving favorable outcomes for both parties.

The Benefits of Outsourcing to Smaller Companies

Outsourcing is a commonly used term in business enterprises nowadays, especially in smaller companies. Come to think of it, if large corporations take advantage of outsourcing to cut production costs, what more in the case of smaller companies? Some of the services outsourced by smaller companies include accounting, payroll processing, and human resources (HR) among others.

But then again, there are still other things to consider in resorting to outsourcing aside from saving money. Such long-term benefits of outsourcing include the following:

(a)   Focus on core business. Looking for a good outsourcing firm can definitely ease away a lot of worries on the part of the business owner. Managers can then put extra attention to strategize on key elements that will satisfy customers and therefore maintain business growth and development.

(b)   Start on new projects quickly. Since most outsourcing firms have all the resources in place, it is easier to start and implement new projects.

(c)   Reduce risks. The ever changing market trends, government regulations, competition and financial conditions can put the business in jeopardy. Acquiring the services of an outsourcing firm can definitely provide solutions to these risks as they are generally much better and experienced in handling such situations.

(d)   Increase in productivity and efficiency. Spending time in doing higher market research and development can be a bit of an issue. Hiring a firm to do all these will give your company more competitive edge.

These are just a few of the countless benefits that small companies can get out of business outsourcing. But then again, choosing the best outsourcing firm should also be prioritized so as to avoid problems that will only lead to unexpected outcomes.

Tips on Choosing the Right Outsourcing Firm for your Company

Outsourcing offers a lot of benefits and choosing the right outsourcing firm for your company is the most critical thing to do. This is because you are about to establish a relationship with a third-party company, a potential partner that can help your business in achieving desired goals and objectives. It is also a must that this firm should work in harmony with your business, observes the same work ethics and as much as possible, follows the same path as yours in obtaining that much coveted success so as to avoid potential conflicts in the future. To carefully evaluate prospective business outsourcing firms, here are some tips that you may want to consider:

(a) Time is gold, even in outsourcing. Before that day comes, you should think ahead and start evaluating possible outsourcing firms for your company. Should there be a need in the future, at least a backup plan is in place.

(b) Be crystal clear on what to accomplish. Outsourcing firms can do a lot for your company but it is still a good thing to lay all the cards on the table. Communicate expectations, discuss costs, and designate project timelines among other business elements.

(c) Product knowledge and expertise matter. Do your homework and research on which outsourcing firms specialize on the area that you want to outsource. If it is payroll, then determine probable choices that will best perform this function for your company. Invest on an excellent talent pool possessing the right knowledge and skills for the job at hand.

Indeed, it would be better to take time in evaluating outsourcing firms. Your company is at stake here so choosing the best partner is highly recommended.

Are US Jobs at Risk due to Outsourcing?

It has been said that on every action, there is an equal and opposite reaction. In lay man s term, this simply means that on every decision people make, there are clear advantages and at the same time underlying disadvantages associated with it. This is very true with the concept of outsourcing.

Outsourcing is very common in business enterprises nowadays. It happens when Company A hires Company B for the purpose of providing services on Company A s behalf. Though the concept may appear to be very simple, there are a lot of things to consider and these include the process of acquiring the services of the best outsourcing firm, among other particulars such as costs, terms and other conditions. Before both companies will come up with an agreement, each should be committed in getting into a partnership in which both parties will benefit from.

But then again, outsourcing drawback was felt way back in 2001. To date, the US appears to have lost more than 3 million jobs because companies are reassigning jobs overseas to save money in production and labor costs. A researching firm, Forrester Research, further indicated that up to US $136 billion in wages will be moved offshore, specifically to countries such as India, China, Russia and the Philippines. The sad truth is 88% of these firms are very much satisfied the way things work overseas, while getting more value for their money. 71% of these firms even pointed out that these overseas workers are even doing more quality jobs. Indeed, this is a bit alarming as outsourcing is definitely here to stay. The US government should act now, before the situation gets even worse.

Tips to Successful Outsourcing Management

The success of the outsourcing partnership between two companies is always dependent on its management. If everything is managed properly, then everything will go as planned. Otherwise, improper outsourcing management could only lead to unmet expectations, costly mistakes and worst of all, project failure.

For proper outsourcing management to take place, here is a list of things that a manager should do (according to industry analysts):

(a)   Keep a copy of the contract. Before it will be signed by both companies, make sure that all terms and conditions are documented. Make sure to renegotiate on costs when there is a need to.

(b)   Decide which party will manage the relationship. Establishing good working relations can definitely lead to a lifelong commitment to excellence.

(c)   When shifting from in-house to outsourcing, it does not follow that the person who previously run business operations is also the right one to do the outsourcing job. There are a lot of undiscovered experts out there and it is a wise choice to let the outsourcing firm decide for you.

(d)   Project success is the determining factor whether processes work or not. Performance metrics should be established to make way for process improvements, if necessary.

(e)   Settle disputes up front and come up with an agreement that is approved to both parties. Maintaining a healthy working relationship is a must before possible problems might arise.

A good outsourcing management in place always means good business. Following these simple tips can definitely result to better client-supplier bondage, producing desired outcomes in no time.

The Advantages of Outsourcing Services Offshore

Outsourcing services have taken business operations not only to greater heights but offshore as well. When cost reduction measures came into the big picture, companies have sought the importance of transferring business functions overseas. Such countries include China, India, Bangladesh and the Philippines, where products are manufactured and services are rendered at a way cheaper price compared to most Western countries where the product or service originated. Aside from being cost effective, some of the advantages of taking business functions offshore include the following:

(a)   Focus. Once a business function is successfully outsourced, expect that the management gets more effective in controlling time. This is because the management has lesser worries to think about, therefore more time is spent on things that truly matters, not only to explore new revenue streams but improved focus on customers as well.

(b) Flexibility. Off load work creates flexibility in the company while ensuring the optimum utilization of available resources within the company.

(c)   Redeployment of company resources. Resources within the company can be used on ways other than performing non-core functions. Once offshore outsourcing is implemented successfully, concentrating on personal strategic issues that require company resources will definitely be prioritized.

(d)   Rapid technological migration.

It is a given that since offshore outsourcing firms are established to support various business functions, expect that these make use of state-of-the-art technologies. This is indeed a plus to the company as there is no need to purchase such technological innovations.

Indeed, offshore outsourcing offers a lot of useful benefits, aside from the fact that these firms operate 24 by 7. Hence, this will surely add more value to clients and its customers as well.

IT Outsourcing   A Better Strategy?

IT outsourcing has always been a big issue, the question of it being an outsourcing strategy is another thing. But then again, this one is for sure. If IT outsourcing strategy is aligned with company business strategies, then everything will fall into place. For IT outsourcing to become successful, an organized and comprehensive view of IT services must be developed. The first step in developing such outsourcing strategy has always been to establish a common understanding of the approach to outsourcing. This would entail the following:

     (a)   Understanding the business value that needs to be provided;

     (b)   Understanding market trends and opportunities;

     (c)   Establishing a common data structure, while optimizing procurement processes and determining potential partnerships;

     (d)   Selecting an outsourcing management model

IT outsourcing solution providers offer such services that include server management, cable management, desktop-client management, website hosting, software license management, connectivity and even IT infrastructure management. This variety of outsourcing options provide more room to a company s IT needs and choosing one that fits can lead to certain innovations that lean towards achievement of individual customer requirements.

It just makes sense that an organization will outsource its IT needs. Why? This is because most business owners and analysts are seeing more value in IT outsourcing. Focusing on what the business and customer needs is always present, while saving on production and labor costs and speeding up the development of business deliverables. Other essential drivers for strategic IT outsourcing include emphasizing on competencies and providing access to new technologies for business growth and development.

Outsourcing   A Brief Introduction

Outsourcing is a contract or arrangement in which one company provides services for another company to be performed by in-house employees that are usually located overseas. This is the trend nowadays and large companies are outsourcing jobs handled by separate third-party companies that specialize in each service. Such services include call center, payroll and accounting, human resources and recruitment among other functions.

There are a lot of reasons why most companies are shifting to the outsourcing trend and these include costs savings, quality improvement and making the most out of the efficient use of technology, labor, capital and resources. If a company has its other services taken care of by another company, it can then focus more on other critical business issues. In addition, outsourcing is a good strategy when it is time for the business to expand. It is also a good way to start building strong relations to other countries.

There also some disadvantages associated with outsourcing. One is that outsourcing prevents a company from building solid relationships with their customers due to lack of direct communication. Another thing is language barrier, which is common to outsourcing call center services. Since most call centers are established outside of the US, many customers find it hard to understand some agents, which may lead to dissatisfaction. Another downside is not being able to control some aspects of the company due to delayed project implementation and communication.

Although outsourcing may prove to be highly beneficial, there are also some unexpected drawbacks. It is very important that companies should think twice and accurately assess if outsourcing is indeed the ultimate solution to the needs of the business.

Some Advantages of Outsourcing: Why Companies Increasingly Go For It

Outsourcing is defined as subcontracting specific functions to a third-party company or -person. An increasing number of companies have begun specific job outsourcing for some basic reasons. These reasons are:

1) to save money or reduce costs,

2) to focus more on the most pressing and/or immediate issues or functions while having external professionals manage other details that need to be taken care of; and

3) to gain access to distinct enterprises or service providers from which they can obtain technical skills and/or services, which are not promptly available within these companies. There are various forms of outsourcing, but the most common forms however are the business process outsourcing (BPO) and Information technology outsourcing (ITO).

On why job outsourcing is increasingly becoming an alternative approach for most companies nowadays is because of the several benefits that companies obtain from doing so. Such benefits include:

1) cost savings since the company gets the outsourced job done by external experts at a reasonable lower cost;

2) better risk and quality control management since the service providers are responsibility in producing certain quantity and/or quality output, which are usually detailed in an agreed upon outsourcing agreement (Service Level Agreements or SLAs);

3) acquiring access to even highly specialized knowledge and expert pools, which may not be available internally and so the company is further enabled to focus on core competencies and

business concerns; and 4) improved management capability since outsourcing provides the company some form of flexibility in managing its production or output.

Outsource service providers may be considered as an additional arm for companies since responsibility for previously done internal functions or tasks are given to them. Unless quality output is consistently provided, a long-term commitment between companies can be possible.

Some Pressing Issues on Outsourcing Jobs in America

Debates on whether or not America continues to outsource its jobs persists. Whether in-shore or offshore, outsourcing is still perceived by many as a national and economic threat than benefit. Economists, American workers, people who label themselves as patriots are but among who are outraged by outsourcing. No one can blame them from their intense reaction as it is possible that outsourcing CAN only lead for Americans to be losing their jobs and therefore, increase in unemployment rate while being substitute by mostly off-shore outsourced workforce.

There is no doubt about the benefits and advantages outsourcing can bring to corporations or among companies of various ranges. However, it is morally devastating enough for American workers to have worked hard educating themselves for job security only to be later deceived and eventually replaced by a continuing off-shore trend. They are asked to even train this new emerging workforce once they have been imported from their country of origin by their companies. Indeed, it is an ill-fated reality. Most of the American workforce exerted to obtain new and more education, improve knowledge and abilities so to succeed in the constantly changing economy. It is a dismal truth however that no matter how they devote themselves to keep up, they realized that these are not enough to contend against the race for corporations to gaining higher profits at cheaper labor costs in the rising global market.

Deliberate movements against outsourcing American jobs are constantly accelerating to make their voices heard. Boycotting outsourced products are among their plans, reinforced by re-educated and re-skilled workers so to become more competent against the new labor force. Americans are not against these rising workforce from developing countries but rather how the global division of labor is being handled.

Outsourcing American Jobs: Issues on Who Benefits More From It?

Although outsourcing jobs can serve as a cost-effective and efficient way for growing and thriving companies to focus more in enhancing core functions and competencies, some outsource-related issues and concerns however, relentlessly increase and continue. The company may have indeed benefitted and will continue to benefit from outsourcing services even so, there may be some unforeseen effects that may later become further pressing matters in the future.

America is among the giant countries that have greatly explored and continues to benefit from outsourcing particularly from third world countries, such as India, China, and other parts of Southeast Asia. There have been, on the contrary, an increasing number of American people becoming pessimistic with regard to contracting jobs. The intentions may be good and rewarding, however, it surprising to know that most of the people who have begun rallying against outsourcing jobs are previous in-house staff.

Unfortunately, outsourcing American jobs has resulted for some companies to gradually lay off their staff or employees. Perhaps these companies have realized and grabbed the opportunity of having their contracted jobs being completely done at affordable costs. Apart from gaining access to specialized skilled workforce, the companies saw some reduction in their operating costs. Another is the fact that maintaining internal employees costs more compared to the cost for an outsourced provider. Outsourcing really does save them time and money, perhaps more than what they have initially bargained for.

For companies to lay off their regular employees and substitute them with outsource providers would result to shaky economic and national security. Where did patriotism go with this scenario?

Anti-outsourcing campaigns are increasingly formed with the aim of representing nothing more than the welfare of the public, particularly of America s once dedicated workforce and their families.

Some Timely Tips Regarding Out-sourcing Articles

Outsourcing is fast becoming the latest trend in many businesses nowadays, especially when it comes to information technology. If you still have not gotten on with the trend (both as a freelancer or as a job provider) then you are really missing out! Do you feel like you are missing on the pertinent information you need to know regarding outsourcing? Fear not, for there are many outsourcing articles that you can read online. Do not know where to start? You can go about this job in two ways. One, you can keyword search on Google anything that you want to learn about outsourcing and once you hit the enter key, you will come face to face with a wide variety of outsourcing articles from different web pages. The second thing you can also do is to visit as many forums as you can and from there you can surf around for interesting outsourcing articles written by average people.

When it comes to looking for outsourcing articles, keep in mind that you ought not to be simply blown away with how great or convenient it is to engage in outsourcing. There are also other factors which you need to consider, factors that will probably influence your decision as to whether or not you really can engage in outsourcing. For one, you need to look for outsourcing articles that tackle the different requirements that outsourcers look for in their freelancers or contractual workers. You need to see if you fit the bill. Another consideration when it comes to looking for outsourcing articles is to see how you and your employee can transact the payment as well as the job submission, as it should be convenient for both parties.

Business Troubles? Outsourcing Consulting is the Answer!

Are you a newbie in the world of outsourcing? While you probably have your own online account, you will probably need a little more help or a bit of wise consulting in how you can outsource the right type of business in order to get the best service and the best kinds of goods. Luckily for you, you can always begin by outsourcing consulting. Outsourcing consulting is a great way to get sound business or information technology advice regarding the business you are in to without actually having to pay a staffer every single working day. Think of it as a cheaper version of hiring a lawyer. When you consult with a lawyer, you pay him or her for the number of hours that the both of you spend together, discussing anything and everything regarding your predicament.

The same goes for outsourcing consulting, although of course, the fees are a lot cheaper! In outsourcing consulting, you will also meet with a respected expert in the field that you are looking into and enlist his help in order to make your project a bigger success. The great thing about outsourcing consulting is that you can only consult on a per project basis and on things that you only need a little bit of help with. Simply look for an outsourcing consultant online, make a background check on his effectiveness as a consultant and schedule a consultation. He will simply need a copy of all the documents you would want him to look into so he can give you the best moves that you ought to take and clue you in on what you should steer clear of.

Reading the Fine Print of Outsourcing Contract

While outsourcing certainly cuts the costs of both service provider and outsourcing professional, there are some things that remain true and traditional despite the lack of an actual work room. One of the true things in outsourcing that is also a familiar fixture in many traditional workforces is that of the outsourcing contract. Since technology dictates how one ought to do the tasks, even the outsourcing contract can be a virtual one virtual but binding as well. An outsourcing contract, when signed by both parties, is a legal document that has repercussions should some clauses in it become violated. So if you are considering doing an outsourcing job, it is highly suggested that you read your document straightaway and look at all the smaller prints.

Before signing your outsourcing contract, you should also get in touch with the prospective client regarding some questions you might have in the contract. This practice is also highly encouraged because it is always better to come up with the questions now than later when the contract is signed. This way, even when your boss is all the way in a Europe or something, you will still have a good working relationship and a commitment to a job you fully understand. Also, it is always best to have a duplicate copy of the outsourcing contract. Never send back the document without keeping a copy for yourself just in case you might want to take another look at it or do something else with it!

Low Outsourcing Costs for Providers and Workers Alike

In the opinion of many people who have found outsourcing as another means of earning a living, outsourcing is a win-win situation for both the job seekers and the job providers. This is because thanks to this newfangled way of working, outsourcing costs have been slashed by almost fifty percent for both parties. On the side of the job seekers, a lot of savings can be placed in the bank since they now work on their own time, wherever they want and however they want. With an outsourcing job, it is time to say good-bye to costly business suits and dresses which are required in a regular workplace (say hello to casual jeans and tee in front of the computer), high priced lunches from the business district where your office is located (time to grab lunch out of the refrigerator) and the rising cost of bus fares or gasoline (get to your workplace, your computer, in just a couple of steps).

On the part of the job providers, there are also a good number of savings they can make thanks to low outsourcing costs. For one thing, they will not need to provide their freelancers or contract workers with health care. Health care is really expensive, and this is not a perk which outsource workers get to enjoy especially if they come from another country. The job providers will not need to hire more staff from an entire department, as maybe two or three staffers will be enough for the company to monitor and arrange for the jobs of the outsource workers. And finally, because there is less people working in a physical space, the company will save on building rents because they will not need such a big space to house all the people who work for them.

Save Time and Money By Outsourcing Data

If you work for a big company (or even a not so big one at that), you ought to know that information is money. Data is important, which is why the realm of research is a multimillion one. For smart business owners, they would of course want to minimize the costs of research in order to tip the scales in favor of profits that they make based on the information they can produce. Which is why many companies and organizations have begun outsourcing data to other individuals who charge lower than industry rates and individuals whom companies will not need to supply any additional employee benefits for (such as healthcare and insurance, for example).

From simple academic research to a full-blown international business research project, outsourcing data is a great way to not only cut the costs of research but to save time as well. If you are a project head or organizer, all you need to do is to hire or outsource someone who can collect the data or the material you will need for your endeavor. This surely beats looking for the information by yourself! To make sure that everything is in place, remind the person you decided to outsource data from to cite all works properly and include bibliography so you can make sure to recognize all the sources of information without worrying about being charged or sued of plagiarism because your worker did not do the legal thing and cite his sources when he worked for you.

Clearly Defining Outsourcing

Since outsourcing is the latest buzz that s been in almost any conversation, almost everyone knows a little bit about it, even down to the minutest detail. To be more exact outsourcing also has its own definition. Accordingly, outsourcing is what you call an arrangement wherein one company will serve to provide another with services. These such services that will be provided can be both common or in house or on the other end, special. By definition alone, we can see that outsourcing is a trend that has only been established in more recent years. It is a trend that is increasingly becoming more common in a lot of different kinds of industries especially in the realm of business and information technology. Outsourcing is also usually regarded as something that is intrinsic to actually managing a business.

There are also some cases wherein companies have chosen to have information management outsourced instead of having it built in their own company. Some of the services they outsource also include the planning analysis and business analysis including the servicing, management and installation of the various networks as well as workstations needed. Outsourcing can also range from the very large contracts such as IBM or something very small like hiring temporary office workers or contractors individually on a regular basis. Whichever the case, outsourcing, as clearly been the method of choice for professionals who want quality work in the soonest possible time without spending a too-hefty sun for it including the different employee benefits and perks.

Double Edged Effects of Outsourcing

Outsourcing has many good and bad effects on people, both service provider and organization alike. Because outsourcing is a recent trend, it was able to replace many established practices and methods in business. Some are actually lucky enough to be able to cope, while some are left with no other choice but to tighten their belts and hope to pass the time until they can gather their bearings yet again. For those who are into the outsourcing sector, especially those who are freelancer, the good effect that outsourcing has on them is on savings. They get to save on money because they can cut down on costs that are usually related to work such as commuting, buying clothes to wear at the office and lunch. On the flipside, working alone will also mean an absence of support from the company. You do not have a business healthcare plan so if you get sick you will have to shell out for your own medicines or hospitalization.

For those who outsource businesses, on the other hand, savings is also a good effect that outsourcing has on them. They do not need to hire additional employees, which means they get to save on employee benefits and also the physical space which the workers of their organization will provide. They will also be easier management of people and systems since they will only need to monitor a token few workers, as well as have multiple tasks completed since they can stop their focus on the work being done outside the office. However, outsourcing will also mean bad news for companies that provide service that same as what is being outsourced, because if this is the case then they might lose their clients to the freelancers.

The Phenomenon of Outsourcing Firms

The greatest thing about the World Wide Web is that it is able to provide a lot of people with great opportunities to make money and to expand their network of connections with others. And many firms saw this phenomenon, which is why they have decided to capitalize on the popularity of this outsourcing trend in the hopes of becoming the medium in which both job providers and freelancers can transact safely and securely. There are many outsourcing firms on the Internet, and all one has to do is to log online and look them up via search engines. The most popular outsourcing firms will be able to offer the freelancer a wide variety of jobs in different industries.

Mostly writing, technical and computer work, the majority of job providers that make full use of these outsourcing firms usually look for individuals who have the skills they need in order to come up with good research work, technical and computer know how and even graphic design as well as typing. These are just some of the jobs that both big and small companies in a different industries delegate to freelancers from outsourcing firms so they can concentrate on more pressing business issues and leave the easy work for those who have the skills to tackle it. Indeed, outsourcing firms are great inventions that allow people to save time, make money and do things more efficiently as well as professionally. Try to look into an outsourcing firm now and get into the trend for yourself!

The Good That Come Out of Out-sourcing

Outsourcing is a godsend for many individuals who are not just cut out for real nine to five office work. Be it writing, researching, fixing computer programs, developing software, making graphic designs, a bevy of individuals were able to make a living out of freelance in outsourcing. This makes outsourcing a good thing, actually. Imagine individuals who cannot commit to a job in an office this does not mean the end of the world for them, because outsourcing is yet another option. Or people who have very low social skills if they lack the panache to interact with bosses and co-employees, they can quietly and efficiently do their work on their own without having to worry about needing to interact with other people whom they might accidentally offend.

Outsourcing is indeed a good thing for many people. Some who do not have the capacity to penetrate the big companies as a regular employee might find outsourcing as a good way to get gratification for his work. One can even make a good name for himself, as companies are also known to refer good workers who provide great service to others. You might not be able to make it big in the regular arena, but that does not mean people will never see you as a professional worker who can provide great service, because you will also carve a niche for yourself in the outsourcing world. The good that comes out of outsourcing knows no boundaries and will not be able to judge people based on a variety of characteristics just plain old service and professionalism.

Tracing the History of Outsourcing

Many people already know that outsourcing refers to accomplishing things from outside the organization rather than delegating work for people inside. What a lot of people are not familiar with is the history of outsourcing in fact, outsourcing is as old as mankind itself. Since the very beginning when individuals began forming groups and groups began forming communities, there were times that the paths of groups crossed in order to avail of services that one could not provide for his own peoples. And that is the most basic definition of outsourcing. In order to overcome the lack of skills, knowledge and efforts, specialization was born and thus, led to what we all know as labor division.

Outsourcing s historical roots may be traced to different times and involves different sectors. To be a bit more official about it, the very first wave of outsourcing can be traced during the time of history when the industrial revolution happened. During this period a lot of services were outsourced the only difference with our globalized time now is that the outsourcing happened within the countryside and not outside of it. The next wave came during the boom of the textile manufacturing industry, where the Indian textile marker began outsourcing their products to the British commercial textile mills. And finally, the third wave in the outsourcing history happened when people started outsourcing the high tech computer items and electronic gadgets via coastal delivery, international and via transactions through the World Wide Web or cyberspace.

Making History with the Outsourcing Industry

one incredibly successful new industry in today s times would be the outsourcing industry. Just to give you a picture of what it really is, outsourcing is a way to get professional service from other people who are not employed in your organization. The more popular term that is on everybody s lips would be the term business process outsourcing, or BPO. This is a great way to serve one s clients while at the same time being able to delegate the work to a lot of companies in the outsourcing industry. For example, the telephone customer contact service sector has been outsourcing such a service to many countries that have a workforce skilled enough to provide English customer support the their many clients.

If you want to know why outsourcing is such a success, it is because many people are realizing that there are enough jobs for everyone. Another reason is that if there are enough people who can cater to the needs of numerous clients from all over the world, then there will be more people bringing in more services and eventually, more revenues. The outsourcing industry is influential enough to spur the creation of many schools that offer long term and short term courses in providing services to the outsourcing industry, as well as skills training and elocution. Clearly, the outsourcing industry is not just life-changing for an individual who has a chance to get a good job, but history-making as well for industries that grow and adapt to the ever-changing times.

Best Information for Outsourcing

If you want to be part of the outsourcing industry, there are some outsourcing information which you need to know in order to see if you can actually hack it or if such an environment will fir your lifestyle and your personality. For one thing, outsourcing is successful if the business process outsourcing company is able to provide services to people in other countries, so if your client is from England, for example, you will need to learn how to speak with a British accent. Meaning, you must be open to studying other languages or at the very least learning the correct pronunciation and lexical terms of your company s clients.

You will also need to have some technical and writing skills, apart from language skills. Technical in the sense that most outsourcing work is done via computers and tele-speakers, so you will need to know how to work your way around a program or a software which will aid you in your work. If you currently do not know how to do this, then a program for such study might work. Additionally, you might need to start adjusting your body clock because you will go to work at abnormal times, usually from early evening to around midnight. The reason for this is because if your client is from all the way on the other side of the globe then you will need to make sure that you can provide services to them at their most convenient time even if it means giving up your own convenience.

An Assessment of Outsourcing in India

The outsourcing boom in India witnesses a lot of activity during the year 2004 until the following year 2005. During this time frame, a lot of ramping up when it comes to the operations of different multinational company players as well as Indian organizations boosted up their hiring. The end result of this was that the domestic business processing market which inevitably catalyzed by the demand from many telecommunications as well as BSFI segments were able to match the growth of business process outsourcing experts. While the market then experienced much maturity as well as consolidation, this also ended in numerous mergers and many acquisitions that took place within such a sector. At that time, there were more than four hundred different companies that operated on the Indian business process outsourcing space, which also included captive units as well as third party providers of services.

The key enabler which allowed this cheaper bandwidth to happen led to lower telecommunications costs for many leased lines, plus a higher availability of educated speakers of English Indians who are part of the Indian business processing outsourcing workforce. Thus, the Indian business processing outsourcing industry then remains to be and a relatively stable growth path as it then emerged as one of the leading key marketable investments in the entire country as well as region. With the entry of information technology major such as 2002 s Spectramind emergence, the business processing outsourcing industry has now become the mainstream factor of the information technology industry in the country of India.

Social And Health-Related Issues of Outsourcing

Outsourcing may be a great way to get back into business, but it is still a serious one with some issues that need to be resolved. One would probably be surprised to learn that most of the issues of outsourcing does not have anything to do with the actual job itself, but the effects it has on the social world. For one thing, family time becomes an issue with a member who is into outsourcing. This is because when a mother or a father (or in some cases, both) work in an outsourcing company, they have to follow the time zone of their clients so if they are providing service to someone halfway across the globe, then they will have to be up late evening till early morning in order to be available for such a client. This simply means that there will be little time to interact with other members of the family at respectable hours since those would probably be spent in rest for the member who is into outsourcing.

Another issue that is also connected to the first one would be health. There are a lot of cases where the health aspect of the employee is affected since it will be difficult for him to adjust his body clock to night time mode, thus making him a bit weaker. Relying on coffee in order to stay awake and alert for the job will also make him prone to palpitations. Providing online and telephone service will also mean being at a desk for long periods of time, thus increasing chances of urinary tract infection.

Great Effects of Outsourcing Jobs to Foreign Countries

Outsourcing jobs are great because it can serve as the bridge that connects the gap between a developed country and a developing one. In a nutshell, outsourcing refers to delegating certain tasks and responsibilities (or services, if you will) to other people for a price. In outsourcing jobs to foreign countries, both service provider and outsourcer will win. This is because when the developed country outsources many jobs to a developing nation, it will be able to save money since generally, labor is cheaper in many developing and third world nations. And to further expand their company, they can use the revenues they saved to open additional business process outsourcing companies in more foreign countries which will then make them more stable and highly regarded in the business world.

On the other side of the bridge, the foreign countries that accept such outsourcing jobs will gain a chance to improve itself both on a national level and a local one. Thanks to outsourcing jobs more people will have a chance to earn good income, so they can provide for their family s basic needs. On the national level, more jobs will mean more purchasing power, so the economy will be uplifted because people will be spending more for their needs, and the different public and private commercial sectors will be able to improve their own sales. All these and more are really thanks to the outsourcing of jobs to foreign countries so it really is a very good thing to actually be part of this trend.

The Good News About Outsourcing Labor

Outsourcing labor is not as easy as it sounds, especially when you are dealing with multinational firms that have a wide reach on an international scale. For one thing, the company that wants to set up an outsourcing satellite office in another country will need to use its smarts to figure out which country has enough skilled workforce to make the outsourcing worth it. They will also need to see if there is enough money to invest in such a project.

On the part of the country where outsourcing labor is to happen, they will also have to choose the location on which the outsourcing company will be set up. There are many prerequisites to this, such as surveys, getting permits, planning their advertising and marketing strategies in order to attract job hunters, and finally choosing just the right personnel for the job.

It is a hard task, one that can only be accomplished by experts and professionals in their respective fields. Luckily, many countries are catching on the outsourcing labor trend, so the effect is that many of their locals are learning how to speak better English as well as equip themselves with the skills necessary to land the job. Making more jobs in a developing country is always good news, so people will be able to live for themselves and uplift the economy at the same time. If any, the trend of outsourcing labor has only been able to spell nothing but good news for anyone who makes himself or herself a part of it.

Latest News Bits in Outsourcing Trends

If you have not been clued in yet, outsourcing is all the rage in many businesses as well as other industries around the globe. The latest buzz in outsourcing news is expanding offices on a multinational basis and targeting the developing countries. Outsourcing news reports that there are many developing countries that actually have very skilled workers especially those who are quick to learn all about the language and pronunciation of the countries they will serve. Currently, many business processing outsourcing countries that come from the United States of America, Europe and Australia are targeting Asian nations to host their outsourcing services.

India and the Philippines are two such Asian countries that fare pretty well in the outsourcing trend. The economies of the two Asian nations have improved in the last eight years, thanks to the influx of business outsourcing jobs that came in from all parts of the world. Not to be left behind, China is now making steady preparations in order to slice a piece of the outsourcing cake for themselves. This is evidenced by the increase of English language lessons in China and many talks between the Asian giant and other outsourcing companies. As it turns out, its direct competitor for outsourcing labor would be India, with both nations going head to head with millions and millions in their work force. The Philippines, on the other hand, remains at a comfortable seat since out of all the nations it has the most effective skills in business process outsourcing.

Which is Which? Outsourcing or Offshoring

Some call it this, while some call it that. In other words, people are easy to mistake outsourcing for offshoring and vise versa. Admittedly, the terms outsourcing and offshoring are interchangeably used in many public conversations without even giving any attention to the very important technical differences between the two terms. The first term, outsourcing, involves getting in touch with a supplier of course, this may, at some degree, be related to offshoring in some sense. This is because offshoring by definition is also the transfer of a function of organization from one country to another, unmindful of the work as to whether or not it is outsourced or if it stays too within the original corporation.

Because of the speedy rise of globalization of many outsourcing companies, there is that distinction which can be found between the two terms outsourcing and offshoring shall be blurred in no time. This is also evident in the ever-growing presence of many Indian outsourcing companies in both the United States and the United Kingdom. Because of globalization of such outsourcing operating models have eventually resulted in newly conjured terms like nearshoring or rightshoring, these too shall reflect the ever-changing reshuffle of locations. Such is also evidenced by the many opening offices as well as operations that are run by Indian companies in both the United States and the United Kingdom. Of course, these might still be well into the future, so for the time being it will indeed be a wise move to actually make sure that one truly knows the distinction between the two.

Great Skill Development in Outsourcing of Jobs

Outsourcing of jobs is really good for people who have not yet found their niche in life. For one thing, the demand for workers in many business process outsourcing is sky high. There are many companies that have lots of opening because they see it is a highly profitable venture and it is really good to be able to provide lots of service to many clients from different countries across the globe. Outsourcing of jobs also does not know any race, gender or age. It is open for people of all ages, for as long as these people are hard-working, driven and know how to discipline themselves. Suddenly, younger ones have a chance to earn decent money for themselves, and older ones who might have been retrenched or in need of a second job have their chance to earn once again.

Indeed, outsourcing of jobs brings many benefits to people who choose to engage in it. even if you decide to move on to a different career path, you will still be able to bring with you the learning you were able to get from your previous job. Conversational skills are top level thanks to the many calls you were able to handle while on the job. Mastering your patient threshold is also an impressive skill. And of course, your ability to multitask is one skill that is highly regarded among all industries what with taking calls, looking at your outsourcing leader, and looking up pertinent call-related information on you computer unit.

Solvable Problems in Outsourcing

While the business of outsourcing and its related industries are indeed a very successful phenomenon in today s business world (especially in the realm of information technology), some problems may also arise every now and then. Luckily for people who operate these businesses, the problems may be seen as easily solvable dilemmas that will go away with time and a lot of forward thinking and wise decision making on their part. For one thing, it is necessary to look for a good country which they need to outsource to. Once they have been able to set their base and settle in comfortably, sometimes some national uprisings (like war and rebellion) will also be influential in the mini economy of business processing offices that opened up in such areas. The remedy? Decide quickly if one thinks it is worth it to stay or better to close shop and pull out.

Another problem would be, of course, the capacity of the systems to deal with the influx of calls, communications and other business matters. Which means their computer systems ought not mess up and fail them, otherwise these companies will end up losing millions in their business. As such, the best thing to do is to invest in the most powerful computers and make very regular maintenance checks on the systems that they use in order to avoid any technological problems which might end up in disaster for their companies. Like it was previously mentioned, these two problems are only easy to deal with if the companies are smart enough to make the right decisions and learn when to stick it out or pull out.

Outsourcing Projects Could Improve Company Financials and Efficiency

Outsourcing projects involve sub-contracting a business process or service to a third party company. Projects here could mean any of the core or secondary functions and processes of companies that they deem more economical and convenient to sub-contract. There are many numerous business processes that could be outsourced. These processes may include IT functions and infrastructure, customer management, human resources, accounting, customer contact or call center functions such as telemarketing, support services, market and business research.

Business process outsourcing has become a standard practice of large multinational and transnational companies. Medium scale industries on the other hand also practice outsourcing projects on selected and few business functions. Some small and start-up companies outsource business processes that they could not management because of capital limitations. These projects may include the IT segment and technology infrastructure deployment or some functions of human resources such as hiring, investigation, and applicant screening.

The most significant impact of outsourcing projects to third party entities is its cost-effectiveness. Companies find outsourcing as a good alternative to cutback on internal overhead expenses and maintenance of personnel and technology. Outsourcing also eliminated the need to maintain redundant business processes. This could streamline the corporate organization and could lead to more efficient business operation. Through outsourcing, companies can focus more on their core processes and competencies. It could also diminish variability on most business process so that these variable functions can be projected as a fixed capital outlay. In the end, companies that outsource some of their business process can achieve financial management stability and optimized operation.

Outsourcing Pros: Two Major Advantages of Business Outsourcing

Outsourcing has many advantages. Most companies today, in one way or another, have outsourced their business processes to third party contractors. The degree of business process outsourcing may depend on the need and financial capabilities of companies. Some companies may have outsourcing projects that could include whole sections or segments of their corporations. While other companies, especially the medium-sized ones, are outsourcing some parts or a small segment of their business operation.

Although outsourcing the business process has many pros and advantages, it all boils down to two major elements. First, outsourcing projects significantly reduces corporate expenses by cutting back on costs of business operations and process. It would be more cost efficient for companies to sub-contract some of their operations and back office support than to maintain it in-house. This is especially true for redundant business operations such as customer support and services, human resources, accounting, and business documentations.

Another advantage of outsourcing is the increased technical capabilities of companies. Some companies have been outsourcing their business applications and IT services needs in order to enhance the technological competencies of their processes and operations. Companies find it more convenient to deploy their information technology infrastructure through third party service providers. These service providers have far better technology and support services for technology architectures. So it would be technologically sound for companies to outsource these services than to build their own technology infrastructure.

These outsourcing pros have contributed significantly in improving corporate financials and capabilities. It is not surprising therefore to see more and more companies resort to business process outsourcing.

Outsourcing Pros and Cons: Is It a Worthy Alternative?

There is a growing trend for companies throughout the world to outsource some of their business segments and back office operations. In fact, business process outsourcing has become one of the most vibrant global industries with expected annual revenues of $20 billion USD. This fact is brought about by the growing sophistication and increasing flexibility of outsourcing companies to provide services to any types of companies.

It would be best however for companies to weigh the pros and cons of outsourcing before trying this business alternative. In this way, companies could really determine if outsourcing would bring benefits to their operations.

The number one benefit of outsourcing business processes is its cost saving effect for companies. Detaching a business segment or part of the company s operation and sub-contracting it to third party companies would reduce operational costs. It also reduces the expenses in maintaining several layers of technical staff and large workforce. Through outsourcing, companies can also allocate valuable resources to other business endeavors and they could focus more on the most important functions of their operation.

On the other hand, companies need to understand that off-loading some of their business processes entail risks. It should be noted that most outsourcing companies today are relatively new. There is a risk of diminishing quality service deliveries if companies will be complacent about its outsourcing projects. Some companies may also experience difficulty in the reduced operational flexibility whenever an innovation has come out. Our sourcing companies may need time to adjust to the innovations thus a company might lose valuable market lead time.

Outsourcing Research: Leveling the Playing Field in Research and Development

Outsourcing research and product development is an excellent option for companies that want to improve their research and development capabilities. Research outsourcing is made possible by the emergence of contract technology providers. These commercial research institutions and companies can provide the necessary technology and expertise in all aspects of product development and research. This development is a significant leap in the business world. It could level the playing field in areas of research making it possible for small and medium industries to compete with huge business organization in product research and development.

In the past, only large companies have definite edge in research and development. This capability created a wide gap between companies. Those that have the ability to deliver the newest technologies, products, and services dominated companies that lack the capability. This created an imbalance and placed medium industries at a disadvantageous position against its bigger competitors. Worse, some companies folded up because it cannot keep up with the latest market innovations.

With the development of research outsourcing, this technological imbalance could be corrected. By utilizing the services of contract technology providers, some companies can conduct their own product development ventures without investing heavily on technology, equipments, and technical expertise. They could easily outsource their research and development needs thus enabling them to introduce product innovations to enhance their market competitiveness. Through contract technology providers, small and medium industries could make their own market impact by delivering innovations. Outsourcing research would revitalize the market and further enhance competition which will definitely benefit the general public.

Some Common Mistakes in Outsourcing Software Development

Outsourcing software development is a common practice today. Most companies contract a third party programming company to write their customized corporate applications. Software development answers the needs of companies in developing their own applications to support their business operations, internetworking capabilities, and database and business intelligence management. It is important to note however that software development is the most complicated and sensitive outsourcing project. Companies therefore need to avoid several common mistakes when outsourcing their software development needs.

Companies need to determine their own organization s needs before contracting a software developer. It would be a waste of time, money and effort if the software would not be very useful for the company s operation.

Another common mistake in outsourcing software development would be to exact impossible expectations on the developer. Of course it is but normal to expect that the outsourced job would perfectly fit in to the specifications of the company. But companies should understand that custom software products will normally develop bugs and other problems. Even giant software companies are plagued by application bugs. So companies that outsource software development should include this in their plans.

Finally, companies need to closely work with the software developer to avoid unnecessary problems. Treating software development lightly would definitely lead to numerous application issues. The process of outsourcing software development should be accompanied by careful planning and close monitoring of project development. In this way, outsourcing software development would not cause much problems and unmet expectations due to lack of coordination with the contracted software developer.

Outsourcing Solution: 5 Important Steps in Contracting an Outsourcing Company

There are many offshore companies that can provide excellent outsourcing solution. Companies desiring to outsource some of their business processes and operations should work closely with offshore service providers. There are five important steps that should be taken before contracting an outsourcing solution provider.

First, companies should carefully analyze their business requirements in order to determine their outsourcing needs. Careful consideration should be done if outsourcing would enhance cost savings and corporate efficiency. These requirements then should be discussed with the target outsourcing company in order to create a common understanding of needs and requirements.

Second, companies must determine their outsourcing model. This is important in meeting expectations and avoiding any problems and misunderstanding with the offshore outsourcing provider.

Third, companies must ensure that they can co-manage the human resource requirements of their outsourced business processes. Most outsourcing companies will allow this in order to ensure that outsourced staffing and manpower hiring would correspond to the standards of parent companies.

Fourth, after the initial processes have been accomplished, companies should sign a definite contract of agreement with the offshore outsourcing company. This will finalize the deal and ensure that both parties will be protected by existing laws and regulations.

Fifth, companies must ensure that they maintain oversight power over the operations of their outsourced business. Outsourcing is not a fire and run business. In order to have a problem-free outsourcing solution, companies must have a degree of control over the offshore unit. This will also ensure that the quality standard set are always implemented by the outsourcing company.

The Benefits of Outsourcing Solutions

Outsourcing solutions provide innumerable benefits to companies. It has become a potent business tool for most companies that seek to streamline their organization and make their operation efficient.

The most important benefit of outsourcing for companies is cost savings. Companies can save on wages and operational implementations through outsourcing. Investments on technological infrastructure and technical support services could also be reduced. The freed resources then could be applied to other productive endeavors or invested in further corporate expansion.

Through outsourcing solutions, companies can access the global skills and talent pool. This access to a rich resource of technical knowledge and expertise could raise the quality standards of company services. By tapping global talent, companies can focus on refining their own strengths and competencies. Another important effect of outsourcing is the significant reduction of business risk to their operations. Offshore outsourcing companies normally take responsibility to the outsourced operations. This is a standard practice and should be included in the outsourcing solutions contract. The reduction of risk is closely associated with improving quality. Outsourcing providers will definitely produce quality products and services because their business is dependent on the continued partnership with the parent company.

Outsourcing solutions are ideal for any types of company. They can easily find an outsourcing provided that will suit their business needs and requirements. The benefits provided by business process and services outsourcing could improve the performance of companies. It could make their operations more dynamic thus improving their competitive edge in the global business environment.

Outsourcing Statistics: Useful Outsourcing Facts and Figures

The most notable figures in any outsourcing statistics report is the continued upswing trend for this kind of business solution. The outsourcing industry has been posting annual growth rates since its inception some decades back. In fact current figures values this robust industry to a staggering $20 billion USD.

The information technology sector has been dominating the outsourcing market grabbing 28% market share. This means that more and more IT companies are outsourcing their software and technology solutions development to offshore outsourcing providers. This development is changing the face of the software development market. The shift in software development to offshore companies resulted to significant workforce cutback in industrialized countries. On the other hand, this development also paved the way for a renewed revenue growth and improvement of corporate financials of most software and IT companies. This shows that outsourcing has a concrete impact on the profitability of the software industry.

This increased financial performance due to outsourcing has led other companies to follow suit. In fact, 40% to 50% of the top 500 companies in the world is leveraging on outsourcing for most of their business processes. These include top corporations not related to the IT sector.

Aside from IT and software development, other business processes that are increasingly being outsourced include marketing and sales, human resources, corporate financials and accounting, customer care and support, and office administration. It has been shown by recent studies that outsourcing these services and business segments could bring a remarkable 50% to 70% savings on the variable expenditures of companies.

Three Business Guidelines before Outsourcing to China

China is seen by most companies as a potential alternative to India in terms of offshore outsourcing. China s extremely huge labor force and relaxation of state regulations made it a solid competitor in the outsourcing industry. In fact, some companies have started outsourcing to China their manufacturing and other business processes. The IT and mobile communication industries are the leading sectors in tapping the domestic talent and work force of China.

When outsourcing to China, companies are generally advised to follow certain business considerations and contingencies. These informal business rules came out as the crystallization of experiences gained by pioneering companies that outsourced some of its business processes and manufacturing to Chinese corporations.

First, when outsourcing to China, companies are generally advised to maintain a certain level of diversity and flexibility in sourcing. This means that companies should find a couple of companies to deal business with. This is due to the fact that some Chinese companies often go bankrupt. The disruption of operation will definitely impact on companies manufacturing and production time table. It is better therefore to consider this before outsourcing to China.

Second, it is generally acknowledge that outsourcing to private Chinese enterprises would be better compared to state-owned and state-subsidized corporation. Although private enterprises in China are smaller they have greater stability and are more flexible in dealing with Western outsourcers.

Finally, companies can use outsourcing as a necessary first step to barge into the huge domestic market of China. Good relations with local businesses could provide companies with a solid partner for distribution and marketing of consumer products. Making it big in the Chinese market will definitely boost corporate sales and production.

Outsourcing to Foreign Countries: Opening New Opportunities for Growth

Outsourcing to foreign countries has opened new opportunities for most companies in industrialized nations. Offloading of business process, manufacturing, and service deliveries to offshore companies have significantly improved corporate financials and productivity. These are due to the intrinsic benefits that a company could get by outsourcing their business segments to a foreign country.

Because of lower wage levels and lower production costs in foreign countries, multinationals and even smaller companies have resorted to offshore outsourcing. Companies can enjoy a marked savings in the overall costs of business operations. This is beneficial to small companies that could not meet the stiff operational expenditures if all of their business processes and services remain in-house. Large companies on the hand can lower their operational costs due to the economy of scale made possible through outsourcing.

Another great benefit that companies can get from outsourcing to foreign countries is the utilization of technical expertise provided by offshore outsourcing providers. Companies would not worry about scarcity of talent because offshore service providers can provide this important human resource. The expertise gained by companies could certainly boost the quality of manufactured products and delivery of outsourced services.

By freeing substantial resources, companies can further develop their core competencies and expand their focus to higher end operations. This will significantly boost economic activity in home countries thus counteracting the fear that off-shoring negatively impacts on the local labor sector. In fact, the increased economic activity due to expansion of higher end operations will create more high paying jobs for the domestic labor market.

Outsourcing to India: Business Segments that can Be Outsourced to India

For many years, India has been a favorite destination of companies for outsourcing their business segments and manufacturing processes. In fact, India continues to be the top choice of most Western companies for off shore outsourcing. This is due to the fact that India possesses a huge labor pool that has superior technical expertise and talent compared to its competitors in the off-shoring industry. When outsourcing to India, people tend to think of the IT and call center solutions only. However, the Indian domestic market has developed in an all-round way making it possible for foreign corporations to outsource almost any of their business operations.

Of course the top outsourcing solution to India continues to be dominated by the IT sector. India has its own silicon valley which is located in Bangalore. Software development and IT engineering and architecture are the foremost outsourcing service that India offer.

Data entry and back office operation can also be outsourced to India. Specifically, services such as data control, auditing, dispatch and validation can be outsourced to India. Important back office operations such as accounting, payroll management, accounts receivable services, claims administration, human resources, and internal auditing among others can be easily outsourced to Indian off-shore service providers. Companies can take advantage of the wide English language proficiency of the Indian work force making it possible to outsource these critical back office and data entry operations to India. This will unload redundant in-house services and will significantly increase the savings of companies in terms of maintaining a back office support.

Outsourcing Trends: Growing Market Means Stiffer Competition

Competition in the outsourcing has become very stiff that countries of offshore outsourcing providers usually intervene to boost competitiveness. There is a growing trend nowadays of foreign countries providing favorable business environments and incentives to outsourcing companies. This is especially noticeable in the current efforts of new players such as China in creating an exclusive business hub dedicated to off-shoring companies servicing corporations of Western industrialized nations. These economic and business zones have the most relaxed state regulations from labor management to almost free tax policies. The trend of providing favorable business environments for outsourcing companies resulted to increased capabilities of countries challenging India s dominance of the outsourcing market.

On the other hand, India has been trailblazing new path for its outsourcing efforts. Indian service providers have developed what they call near-shoring operations. This is a counter measure which will try to attract investors by providing the facilities of outsourcing companies near the parent company. Near-shoring has been developed by European companies specifically capture the large and cheap labor pool of former Eastern European states. India made it a strategy to generate more clients for its outsourcing companies. Near-shore facilities, will significantly cut the parent companies expenditures in terms of management cooperation, product deliveries, and service provision.

The outsourcing industry is growing from year to year. It has become a major industry in some countries that fuel local economies and market. The current trend now is increasing innovation in service deliveries to capture more companies that will outsource their business operations.

Make Outsourcing Work through These 3 Basic Tips

Outsourcing is a powerful business tool that can be used to significantly enhance profitability, savings, and efficiency. There are good practices that companies can emulate to make outsourcing work for their benefit. Making outsourcing work will certainly improve corporate performance and will open new opportunities for growth.

First, outsourcing should not be a hire and forget event. It should be pointed out that companies must continue to exercise control and macro management of the providers operations. Although the outsourcing provider is generally responsible for quality deliveries, safety, and maintenance of product and services standards, parent companies must ensure that all these are being followed by offshore companies. This would further reduce risk, wastage, and serious quality issues.

Second, it would be best to establish good working relation-ship with an outsourcing provider. This can be made possible through effective communication, appointment of regular liaison, and allowing flexibility to some business practices. Although the outsourcing market provides numerous options, it would still be difficult to establish relationship with a new provider. Shifting from different outsourcing providers could disrupt normal business operations. Contracting new providers also will take time which could affect other corporate segments. So it would be ideal for companies to try to stick to an outsourcing company and maintain good business relations with them.

Finally, companies must negotiate the best service level agreement that is flexible and can accommodate major changes in the nature of outsourcing operations. The SLA must also integrate a viable exit plan that will clearly define details of contract termination.

The Advantages of Getting Into Payroll Outsourcing

Who would have thought that even company payroll services will be outsourced too? It seems that almost any business function has a corresponding outsourcing firm to match every needs of the company. And to top it all, most of these firms are located overseas. But what are the reasons behind such a shift in business operations? Here are some of the benefits of outsourcing payroll:

(a)   Reduce costs. This seems to be always present when outsourcing benefits are being talked about. Processing payroll can be greatly reduced by working with a payroll service provider.

(b)   Avoid dealing with IRS Penalties. Incorrect and late filing of payroll leads to a major disaster. Payroll services usually provide a more consistent payroll scheme, ensuring zero IRS fines.

(c)   Focus on things that truly matter. Since payroll processing is time consuming, acquiring the services of a third-party firm can free up production time. This also means that income-generating activities will be more prioritized.

(d)   No wore worries. Dealing with payroll services is not only tiresome but mentally draining as well. Outsourcing payroll will definitely ease all the pain of having to get through all those figures, paper works and documents.

(e)   Control outside payroll expertise. Changes in government regulations, withholding rates, tax status and salary increases can be easily taken care of by an outsourcing payroll service provider.

Payroll outsourcing is indeed a company strategy that every business owner should think about. It does not only provide practical benefits but it is also a great way to eliminate stress at the work place.

Procurement Outsourcing: Reducing Cost of Production and Improving Quality

Procurement is a key element of company operations. Sourcing of materials for the production process and finding the right supplier offering the best deals and quality is very important to company profit margin management and growth. Unfortunately, some companies suffer form inefficient and ineffective procurement services methods which could leave them vulnerable to losses and decreasing profit. This will compromise the stability and commercial viability of companies. Because of these situations, more and more companies are resorting to procurement outsourcing.

Procurement outsourcing is the transfer of the key procurement processes to a third party contractor. The outsourcing partner will be responsible for finding the best supplier and supply chain for the client in order to optimize the supply management, increase the profit margin, and reduce loss vulnerability. Companies with poor performing procurement processes and services are taking advantage of the expertise and technology provided by outsourcing companies. Procurement outsourcing companies dedicate their efforts and resources solely in finding the correct match of suppliers for companies. This places them at an ideal position to boost this important enterprise activity. It will therefore improve the commercial viability of companies because of increasing reduction of costs associated with supplies procurement and the assurance that only quality raw materials would be utilized for the production and manufacturing processes.

Through procurement outsourcing companies can leverage their efforts in fine tuning their manufacturing practices. This will significantly improve product quality standards. Improved product deliveries will, in the end, be transformed to significant corporate performance, productivity and profitability.

What are the Pros and Cons of Outsourcing

Outsourcing has many pros and cons. However, this is natural because every business endeavor or solutions has its own advantages and disadvantages. The key is how to leverage the pros of outsourcing in order to neutralize or even eliminate its cons or disadvantages.

First, outsourcing is an effective cost saving measure. It significantly reduces expenditures and lower in-house operational cost. By outsourcing business segments and operations, companies can save on resources that will be devoted to wages, technology solutions, IT infrastructure, energy requirements, and technical expertise. Companies can also increase their productivity through outsourcing.

Offshore outsourcing makes it possible for companies to manufacture and deliver products and services for twenty four hours. This is especially true if the offshore location operates on different time zones. So production and deliveries will not stop without paying additional overtime pay to workers. This significantly enhances productivity and profitability. By freeing resources and staff efforts, companies can concentrate on improving their main business functions. This could raise the standards and quality of their higher end business operations.

On the other hand, outsourcing entails risk such as loss of control for some business operations. Through outsourcing, some company trade practices can also be compromised thus losing an advantage over its competitors. The local labor market is also highly disgruntled by companies outsourcing their business processes. This could lead to labor unrest at the home front which could be very detrimental to the company s operations.

Before deciding to outsource, companies are generally advised to weigh their options if the benefits of outsourcing will be greater than its disadvantages.

Recruitment Process Outsourcing: Finding the Right Employees for Companies

Probably the most outsourced back office support and service is human resources. Specifically, hiring new employees is the most common human resource aspect that is being transferred to outsourcing companies. The recruitment process is probably the most intricate and elaborate segment in human resource management. To offload this HR segment and free its human resources staff to more critical tasks, companies are contracting third party talent solutions specialized to supply them with qualified employees.

Recruitment process outsourcing brings a superior system to the hiring procedures of companies. Service providers of human resource management offer industry best practices in talent pooling, screening, and hiring. Recruitment processes outsourcing providers could easily scour the labor force and find the most suitable candidates for the company s personnel requirements. It significantly enhances retention and optimization of employee talents.

Recruitment process outsourcing providers can also speed up the hiring process thus eliminating the risk of long term disruption of work and under staffing. The speed of recruitment can also impact on productivity which is beneficial to company productivity. Recruitment process outsourcing will therefore improve the company s hiring schedules which could be critical especially in urgent projects or critical business operations. The best recruitment outsourcing provider should work closely with the company s human resources department. This will improve common language and understanding of the requirements needed by the company.

The ability to work with recruitment process outsourcing provider will enable companies to reduce unqualified hiring and fast turn-over of employees. In this way, companies can enjoy continuity and uninterrupted operations of important business segment.

Sales Outsourcing: Widening the Customer Base of Companies

Corporate sales are probably the most vital aspects of its commercial viability. Decreasing sales mean losing money, while improving sales figures signify a robust market performance and naturally increasing profit. It is therefore important for companies to improve their sales performance in order to maintain its operation. However, most companies are lacking the resources and facilities to breach new market and new customer base. This could be solved by sales outsourcing. Companies could contract a third party to help them break into new market areas and find serious sales leads. These leads could be a good start in creating new customers that could boost the client base of companies.

Specifically, sales outsourcing companies have the necessary personnel and expertise in generating new accounts and new customer leads. Companies then could convert these leads into serious buyers and partners thus improving sales performance and overall profitability. Usually, sales outsourcing companies have their own different exclusive territorial coverage where they exercise market influence. They also have dedicated sales teams that will push their client s products and services. They could also offer consumer win back programs that could entice new customers to patronize the products of their clients. All these have been developed through long years of sales outsourcing services they provide.

Sales generation is a critical part of the business process. If this aspect of the company s operation will not improve, the overall profitability and viability of its operation will suffer major losses. These then could impact on the entire company operation. Through sales outsourcing, this weakness could be arrested. The service provider could turn around fluctuating profit and bring back company operations to its feet.

Why Use Software Outsourcing?

Small companies want to be successful in their business ventures at lower costs. They cannot compete with big businesses in terms on technical expertise. But there is a way to be able to access software without much cost this is to use software outsourcing. This can help companies save time and money while concentrating more on the core functions of the company.

A company needs to have software that is reliable, compatible and secure. Software outsourcing can provide this. Here are a few reasons why a company should use software outsourcing:

1. One of the primary reasons is that expertise in software is outside a company s major functions. Therefore, it is more practical to hire a company that knows more about this and has the available resources and experiences needed. Moreover, this shall also help the company to manage its time, money and efforts to more important business functions.

2. It takes time to get expert developers because these are specialized jobs. A fast solution is to get a software outsourcing company that can start the project immediately. There is no need to worry about hiring or training in-house staff. Moreover, your existing in-house staff can learn from the expertise of others.

3. A company can also avoid the small headaches associated with organizational delays due to clashes and leadership changes. A software outsourcing company is free from internal problems and therefore can focus on the main functions needed to be done.

Software outsourcing can be especially beneficial to small businesses that have limited resources for software. Resources are better concentrated to make the core functions a success this can make a big difference on the business.

Strategic Outsourcing: A Powerful Business Solution for Every Company

More and more companies today are making outsourcing a strategic business solution. Some of the biggest and most successful multinational corporations made strategic outsourcing as a core tool in operating their global business. Through outsourcing, these giant companies have significantly improved their productivity and profitability. They also dominated the world market by focusing more on their business strengths. Outsourcing also upped their first to market performance especially in the field of product innovation and development. These tangible and intangible benefits that they get from strategic outsourcing contributed greatly to their continued competitiveness in the global business environment.

Strategic outsourcing can also be used by small companies who have limited operations. It could also serve as a strategic tool to improve their market performance. By outsourcing some if not most of their business operations and princesses, companies can improve their cost savings measures. The significant savings they can get will free valuable resources which could be used for other productive purposes. Their in-house talents can also focus more on their primary business competencies because they will be unburdened by redundant business operations.

Outsourcing as a strategic tool also can improve the market position of companies. If they will be unfettered by other business operations, staff and experts can focus in developing new marketing strategies which could improve their sales performance. If sales could be improved, this will definitely mean increasing profit and continued company growth. Companies that made outsourcing as a strategic business solution show bullishness in the otherwise uncertain market. This shows that outsourcing could really boost businesses and increase commercial competitiveness.

Technology Outsourcing: Practical Guides for Small Businesses

One of the challenges of small-businesses is to be able to manage its own information technology infrastructure ranging from e-mail servers, firewalls, and virus protection and computer stations. For a company who has no in-house experts on these matters, this can be a big problem. The obvious solution is to hire experts but this can be very expensive. You can train your in-house staff but these takes time and can be expensive. Moreover, it can also be a source of conflict among your employees as these are additional functions. What can small companies do then? They can look outside the company and consider technology outsourcing.

This set-up is much more affordable and convenient. But companies have to choose the best technology outsourcing company. What should a company look for? First, make sure that the company is offering services that are more preventive and pro-active. This means that the company are concerned to prevent problems and are not just reacting to it. Also, this company shall ensure that your data are backed up, that spyware are always restricted and anti-virus is updated. Second, ask the outsourcing company if they are on-call 24 hours a day and 7 days a week. If not, a company must find one that offers these services. Third, the company must find out whether the outsource company has good engineers that can regularly check on your systems. Fourth, the company must check on the experiences of the provider. What are the companies that they have served?

A company must make an extra effort to find a good technology outsourcing company that fits to the need of the company. If its possible, a company can avail of a free needs assessment from the outsource company to help in the final decision of choosing a partner.

Who Benefits from US Outsourcing?

To an average person, US outsourcing seems to be a waste of time, money and effort. It might seem to be a complicated set-up when there are available human resources that can provide such services in their own country. To a politician, it is an issue that he can use to make a point towards nationalism that being US companies should provide jobs for their countrymen. There are various negative reactions to US outsourcing. However, for a businessman, this is like manna from heaven. US businesses are the first beneficiaries of outsourcing.

They can outsource other functions that are not core functions of the company to other companies overseas such as financial and administration, human resources, customer services and accounting services. The functions are important but outsourcing them can produce better results in terms of cost-reduction and quality services. Moreover, small US businesses also benefit from the outsourcing scheme especially if they lack the expertise to implement software administration or accounting functions.

The second beneficiary of outsourcing is the country where the outsourcing company is based. These countries have many highly intelligent graduates but no job opportunity available. Outsourcing therefore is a good opportunity for them to earn comparable salaries in their countries without leaving their home. Outsourcing is a win-win situation for both US businesses and outsourcing companies from overseas. The US companies provide salaries that are lower compared to the standard salaries in the US whereas the employees from outsourcing companies are quite satisfied with their salaries, which are higher in their country s standards.

The debate over the effects of US outsourcing continues among politicians and economists. On one side is the argument that free trade which includes outsourcing benefits US businesses and its citizenry in the long run due to gains from free trade. Whereas on the other side is the fact that US are losing white-collar jobs to outsourcing companies.

What is Outsourcing: Some Basic Information

Outsourcing is a business practice or a process of transferring certain corporate operations, processes, and business segments to a third party contractor. This may be considered subcontracting but outsourcing is a broader concept that could encompass not just a single project but also an entire business operation. Outsourcing has been practiced for many decades now. Today almost every major company is outsourcing parts of their business operations mostly to offshore companies.

Outsourcing first started as an IT solution. Some companies are finding it more difficult to provide in-house IT service support and development. The profitability of the IT segment is diminishing if it remains an in-house operation. This development pushed many companies to outsource their IT requirements which include important programming and software development. With this practice, companies observed marked improvement in their corporate financials. Specifically, companies experience greater cost benefits through outsourcing. It significantly reduced operational and maintenance expenses and improved profitability. Until today the IT sector is the most outsourced business operation. It dominates the outsourcing industry by getting 28% market share.

On the other hand, outsourcing has become a viable solution for companies to offload some of their business operations not related to IT segment. Back office operations, accounting, administration, financials, and human resources are being outsourced to third party entities. This further boosted the global demand for service providers that can absorb redundant operations of companies. Today, outsourcing providers continue to post significant growth rates. But because of increasing demand, competition is also getting stiffer in the outsourcing market.

Why Outsource: 4 Compelling Reasons Why Companies Should Outsource

There are four reasons why companies should outsource their business operations, processes, and production.

First, outsourcing can bring many financial advantages. It is surely a very good cost savings measure. The cheap labor cost associated with outsourcing can increase company savings. The technology requirements of companies which could be provided by third party contractors can also add to the savings. Increasing company savings can definitely improve company financials. This improvement will therefore impact on the profitability of companies.

The second compelling reason why companies should outsource is the availability of technical expertise and competence of outsourcing companies. This will improve company capability in creating superior products and services. This will also improve the development of new products and innovative services which could enhance competitiveness.

Reduction of risk is another reason why companies should outsource. Normally outsourcing providers are primarily responsible for delivering quality products in the most efficient manner. It is usually stipulated in the Service Level Agreement that outsourcing companies shall make sure that the products and services of parent companies will conform to specified standards. There is a penalty for non-conformance. This therefore reduces the risk of business operations especially in the manufacturing and service delivery sector. If risks are reduced, companies can fully focus its quality efforts on higher end business operations.

Finally, companies can now perform critical research and development ventures to improve their products. This is made possible by outsourcing research to third party research institutions. The expense associated with research and development could be significantly reduced. This is highly beneficial in introducing innovations which could make companies more competitive.

Printed in the United Kingdom
by Lightning Source UK Ltd.
130743UK00003B/181/P

9 780980 497168